Untranslatable

Katherine Elizabeth Walsh

Eliezer Tristan Publishing
Portland, OR

Cover design by Shari Ryan

For Ginny Leary and Lauren Herman,
Who knew this book would happen, years before I did.

The spotted hawk swoops by and accuses me, he
complains of my gab and my loitering.
I too am not a bit tamed, I too am untranslatable,
I sound my barbaric yawp over the roofs of the world.
The last scud of day holds back for me,
It flings my likeness after the rest and true as any of the
shadow'd wilds,
It coaxes me to the vapor and the dusk.
I depart as the air, shake my white locks at the runaway
sun,
I effuse my flesh in the eddies, and drift it in lacy jags.
I bequeath myself to the dirt to grow from the grass I love,
If you want me again look for me under your boot-soles.
You will hardly know who I am or what I mean,
But I shall be good health to you nevertheless,
And filter and fibre your blood.
Failing to fetch me at first keep encourages,
Missing me one place search another,
I stop somewhere waiting for you.

Leaves of Grass by Walt Whitman 'Song of Myself'

Contents

Part one

Essays in My Mind

First Day of Life

TODAY, I HAVE RECEIVED three text messages asking me if I am okay. I am alone today. The last day I was alone I was sitting on the living room floor with a knife to my arm trying to etch out my exit strategy. I spent the next few days in the psych ward where I was followed around by a crack addicted schizophrenic who talked with stolen food spilling out of her mouth about how I was heaven because of my blue eyes. Today, I sit with the cats and my copy of *Love Warrior* ready to take on the world. Am I okay? Yes, I believe I am.

Glennon Doyle Melton writes that we, the ones who suffer from our mental illness, are like the canaries that they would send down the mine shafts in order to detect poison. Through our suffering, our too much feeling-ness, we warn the others of the poison in life. I like this. I like the idea that I am little and yellow and a warning. That through my bleeding and food issues, I am not broken. I am in fact standing up to life and saying, "Hey, here's the poison and we are not all 'fine'."

During my stay, I tried really hard to stay away from people. Stayed in my room, read books. One of the nurses was not having it. It is also a teaching hospital. Every time the students came onto the ward, this nurse would hunt me down and tell me to sit and talk to the students. Later, he sat me down and asked me why I thought he did that? I told him I thought it was because I was one of the only people who could have a regular conversation. He looked at me, told me, "No. It's because I think you spend a lot of time by yourself and I think you are a very angry person. A person who isn't angry doesn't cut their arm open like that. You are angry, and you pretend that everything is fine all the time. You know how I know THAT? It's your eyes. When you smile at people, it doesn't reach your eyes. Your eyes look completely dead." This nurse blew my mind. He didn't know me at all, except he did. He was paying attention way more than anyone else in my life had. He knew things about me I was just starting to learn about myself. It freaked me out and really caused me to have a good sit down with myself and toss over the idea that maybe I wasn't doing that amazing of a job pretending to be what I wasn't: happy, joyous, and free.

My brother told me that he is in the end stages of grieving my life. That he expects a phone call one day saying I am dead, and he is no longer saddened by this thought, he just expects it. I am not willing to grieve my own life. I am here, and I am ready to stand up and fight for it. I want to surface from the water I have been drowning in, break the glass that separates me from the rest of the world, and live.

Really live. Meet people half-way, show up for myself and everyone else. This is the first day of my life. I am ready.

Gentle Disassociation

MY THERAPIST TELLS ME after every session to 'be gentle with myself' and I always think. What does that mean? Today, it means get up, drink coffee,[1] eat (even though I don't want to) and do yoga (even though I really don't want to).

Yoga is the type of thing to get you in your body. I hate this. I hate the resurfacing when I am happy floating in my little water world. I often times feel like Sebastian from *The Little Mermaid*, "The human world, it's a mess'. Why would I want to rejoin this? Well, because it is crazy and messy just like I am, and everyone of us - even me - needs to wake up, show up and embrace the mess. I have spent a long time thinking that because I am a mess, I do not fit among the world at all. This is one of the lies I tell myself. If I actually took about five seconds to think about this lie, I would know it is not true. If I am a mess and the world is a mess, how on earth do I NOT fit into it perfectly? The

---

[1] *I drink coffee every day. I'm not sure who I think I'm kidding with that one.*

answer, of course, is that I do fit. I fit very well. When I stop trying to not fit, I find other people who feel like they don't fit. Like we have a gravitational pull towards each other. The moment we admit to some of our mess, it is met with a 'oh yeah, I get that and feel that a lot of the time'. The more I think about it, why would I not want to be part of the mess? Mess can include: art, baking, cooking, shuffles of papers begging for words, digging in the dirt to help something grow. Oh my God. *Mess is how we create anything.* I figured that out just this moment, seriously. I know it gets said in other ways. Ways that are all prophetic and dreamy. Think about it! You cover your kitchen in flour and sugar, at the end you get cookies, and cookies are great! You spend time getting covered in paint, or dirt, or ink, and then something new, something that has never existed before, is made. How cool is that! The mess creates something the entire world has never seen! I'm a very slow learner. This is going to keep happening, I will keep getting excited about new things that have actually been said to me over and over again. Just not in ways that fit with my mind.

As the Goddess Brene Brown says, "You are imperfect and wired for struggled and you are worthy of love and belonging." I, too, am imperfect and wired for struggle and so worthy of love and belonging. Being gentle on myself is knowing and accepting this love and belonging. Loving and accepting myself and loving and accepting other people.

So today, just for today, for this moment; I will be gentle to myself. I will do the next right thing and I will accept my own love and belonging. I will rise from the pool of my own mind and join the world. I will meet people where they stand. Today, I will show up for myself.

All I Need

TODAY I AM REMINDED of something as I coach the family dog[2] down the stairs. He is afraid of the stairs and will endlessly stand at the top of them barking until help has arrived. As I stood there turning on the light, telling him he does in fact have help and everything he needs, I realized that the same applies for me in my recovery. I, too, have everything I need; the light is on and help has arrived.

Today in my meeting, we talked about step three. Which is hard for me. Hard because I am far behind. I am on step 0.5. I have control issues, surprise surprise. So, the thought of surrender is hard for me. For someone with a history of sexual trauma, the word surrender has not ever meant something good. It has meant surrendering myself, giving up in order to survive.

While sitting there in the meeting, I thought about how selfless I thought I was. I'm a good person; I help others and volunteer my time when I can. Then I realized that in my suffering I have made myself the higher power. Every

---

[2] *This dog has since died. My mother turned him into garden stones.*

time I slam myself in the psych ward, every time I need the attention drawn to me, I am causing the greater being to be me. This is selfish. Not because I am in the psych ward or needing attention, but because I am not asking for help before it happens. I am not taking steps to not get here again. Instead, the worse I feel, the more I try and help other people. After all, there are A LOT of social media posts telling me that if I help others I will stop feeling so shitty.

So, as I journey on this new path, I will remind myself to check my ego. Not because I don't need my ego. I do. My ego is the thing that tells me to look out for myself. That I am important enough to be looked after. To ask for help even, and to also look out for other people. Only after I have taken care of myself. For today, just for today and this moment, I will remember that the light is on and I have everything I need.

I Love You... Now Change

WHEN I WAS IN the psych ward the last time (the same time I was told I had dead, fish eyes), I was given an assignment to list twenty things I love about myself and 10 things I want to change. At first I thought this an impossible task until I was told to keep it simple. Did I love that I could walk? Yes. What about my hair? Yes. My teeth? My eyes? Yes. Yes. I decided to write out my list.

20 Things I Love About Me
1. I love my blue eyes
2. I love my game. I got the girl, baby!
3. I love my hair
4. I love my teeth
5. I love my supportive family
6. I love my mobility
7. I love my tattoos
8. I love my sense of humor
9. I love my freckles
10. I love that I can afford to not work because I worked hard before, so now I can focus on me

11. I love that I can read
12. I love that I can hear
13. I love that I know American Sign Language
14. I love that I can see
15. I love that I went to school for theatre
16. I love that I wake up every morning knowing I have food and a place to live
17. I love that I can memorize things quickly
18. I love that I'm in an A cappella group
19. I love my experiences
20. I love that I took care of my grandmother

10 Things I Want to Change About Me
1. My anger
2. How internally mean I am to people, including myself
3. I take things for granted
4. My self-hatred
5. My victim mentality
6. My depression
7. My inability to ask for help, and accept it
8. My self-sabotaging behaviors
9. My inability to show emotion
10. My stubbornness

After creating these lists, I realized there was so much more that I loved about myself than hated. It took so much less time to create the twenty than it did the ten, and I was pleasantly surprised and encouraged by this assignment. I have also encouraged other people to do this.

Slowly, start with the things they like. Oh, how hard is it for people to come up with things. It is so easy to completely complicate this activity. To sit and stare at a blank page, trying to come up with twenty really amazing, inspired, enlightened things about yourself. That's a terrible way to start. In the journey of learning to love ourselves, simple is the best tactic. You don't have to be the second coming of anyone. Maybe it is enough to love all the things we take for granted. Millions of people in the world cannot read. If you are reading this, there is your first thing you can love. You have the ability to look at a jumble of random symbols and translate them into your own language. No, not maybe, I *know* that is enough. That is some small magic working. Maybe also love that you are magic, because you are.

Today, just for this moment, I will remember that there is so much of me to love. I am a work in progress. I am growing and changing every day, and I love that I have the ability and tools to do so.

The Victories

RECOVERY IS NOT so simple as 'just eat'. It is about finding a new purpose in life away from the eating disorder, it is about learning to love your new body. All of these are very hard things. I have spent so much of my life doing nothing but my eating disorder. Every moment consumed by it, and my days were so much longer then because starvation meant I didn't sleep. Every single day was dedicated to numbers (weights, scales, calories consumed and burned), writing those numbers down, adding and subtracting. The numbers were the hours of exercise, the amounts of diet pills. I often would not go out and socialize for fear that food would be involved. I find it's really hard to plan the lie of why you aren't eating if it is a surprise. Too often, the night ended with me passed out on the floor. I did not have time for anything else. When your brain is packed full of your eating disorder, you aren't a person any more. I had to spend energy I didn't have on creating the perfect image of myself. So everyone would like the shell of me, not the real girl.

As I begin the process of learning to find my purpose, I find that I am spending a lot of time really doing nothing. However, is it nothing? Every day that I don't engage in an ED (eating disorder) behavior is really a win for me. Every day I choose to eat my three meals and don't purge, I am choosing recovery; I am choosing life. So maybe that's not nothing. Maybe that's winning and doing the most important something there is to do[3].

While I feel day in and day out that I should be using my time to do something extraordinary, I am beginning to realize that maybe I am. Could it be that being in recovery moment to moment is the extraordinary thing that I am doing? And I am doing it most every day. I say most every day because I am human, and I have my slip ups. I have my days where I want to restrict or purge, and even the days where I act on these things. However, I know they are just moments now. Not my life. And as I strip away the eating disorder, I am discovering me. Discovering the me I am meant to be and my purpose on this journey.

Today, just for today, just for this moment, I will allow myself the victories[4].

---

[3] *Spending all day crying over* Grey's Anatomy *some days isn't nothing either. It's facing emotions with doctors.*

[4] *And just one more episode of* Grey's Anatomy. *I swear.*

The New Year

WHILE I DON'T BELIEVE in resolutions, I do feel that I am always healing and always beginning my journey new each day. So, in that vein, my focus is going to be on Love. Accepting it more from other people, and more importantly, accepting it more from myself. I think that is what life is about anyway. We are put on this earth to figure out how to endure Love.

In doing so, I hope that my mind and body can not only be a place where I have accepted to live in, but that they also become places I love living in. To love other people and myself more fiercely and passionately every day.

So, for today, just for today, just for this moment. I will accept and receive love from myself and other people with gracious and open arms.

Happy New Year!

Gym Musings

THIS MORNING, MY MOM wanted to go to the gym. My dad swiftly looked at me and said, "Get off your ass and go get a gym membership. Go DO something." Now, as a person in eating disorder recovery, this was not the thing I needed to hear. Millions of not-enough thoughts swam through my head and tears ran down my face as I got ready for the gym: 'I am too fat', 'I am too ugly', 'I am too lazy', 'I am simply not good enough', 'Fat, Fat, Fat, Fat'. I also should point out that I am very anti-exercise. After years of over-exercising, I have decided that I am allergic to exercise and try very hard to avoid it at all costs.

Upon arriving at the gym, the overly chipper employees at the front desk met me to sign me up. In my vulnerable state, I was feeling judged by them. Their upbeat attitudes were a little much, smiles a little too forced. After what seemed like a year, I was finally all signed up and ready to take on the gym. Of course, the first thing I did was go to the scale and weigh myself. Although that number wasn't as bad as I expected, I proceeded to have the next hour be ruled by numbers; the amount of calories I was burning, the miles I was going, my pace.

I turned on the Hamilton soundtrack and switched the TV to a southern cooking channel. Nothing like American history set to song and a smiling blonde lady cooking with butter to motivate you to work out. Just shy of twenty minutes in, I was wondering if the girl in front of me, who was actually working out - not just slow walking like I was - would be my friend. We already had a love of Grey's Anatomy[5] in common. What more do we really need? The southern lady and her friends were now spraying canned cheese into their mouths and beaming at me from the TV (how is this a cooking show?). I did have about 2 minutes of feeling motivated when the song *Hurricane* started playing; "I wrote my way out of hell, I wrote my way to revolution, I was louder than the crack in the bell". This was very motivating, briefly.

By minute twenty-two, I was bored and busied myself with looking at everyone else coming in and out while keeping my eye on my new best friend, Grey's Anatomy Girl. She was brilliant, really a pillar of health. She came to the gym to actually work out and watch her favorite program. I, however, had only walked 0.6 miles and burned way fewer calories than I thought I should have at this point. That's when I decided the only possible explanation was that my machine must be broken. No way could I be this sweaty and have made such little progress. Grey's Anatomy Girl did

---

[5] *See! I knew* Grey's Anatomy *would come in handy. No, we never became friends. Talking to strangers is creepy unless it's through the internet.*

cause me to have a revelation; the gym was a good excuse to watch TV in the middle of the day. No one would tell you not to binge-watch Netflix if you were moving your feet at the same time. Brilliant! While today started in tears, I now have an excuse to watch TV in the middle of the day, blast music, and not talk to anyone for a little while. I could get used to that.

Today, just for today, just for this moment, I'm going to remember that I have dedicated myself to Love and will try and love myself and my body for even being able to go to the gym, even if I'm still allergic to it.

The Miracle

TONIGHT, INSTEAD OF picking up the razor to cut, I picked up lotion to put on my body. Instead of heading to the bathroom to purge, I lit a candle. There is a saying in recovery: 'Don't give up until you get the miracle.' I realized tonight that you and me, the warriors in recovery, we are the miracle.

We fight every day even when people don't see it. We stay up late because we are fighting and go to sleep early other nights because we are so tired from the fight of the day. So, for all of you out there fighting, I want you to know I see you.

Because when I gave up my eating disorder, I lost who I was and am still trying to get who I am back. Because if I'm not hurting myself or being hurt by others, I don't know how I'm supposed to be treated. Because I am so tired of the fight that no one sees and want you all to know that the fight in me recognizes the fight in you.

I love you, keep going.

Adventures of an Ice Queen

DURING ONE SESSION of DBT therapy, while in residential treatment, my recovering bulimic therapist warned me that if I didn't stop purging, eventually when I went to bed at night or woke up in the morning, my nose would fill up with acid and I wouldn't be able to breathe. I thought this was another bullshit-can't-happen-to-me-thing. Well, it happens now. Not only can I not breathe but it causes me to throw up. The things they don't tell you before it is too late. Or like how if I eat too much or drink something bubbly, I am also at risk of throwing up. Warm beverages cause this to happen sometimes too. Does anyone else sometimes bend over the wrong way or hit something in their mouth while brushing their teeth and… oops, vomit again? My blood sugar also drops so low in the morning some days that I wake up shaky and puking. Since I am human, I still get very mad at myself. I wanted my eating disorder so badly that I did not listen to any warnings. I also really did not know a lot of this was going to be a side effect. The information I wish I had. That's fooling myself though, I was never going to listen.

I am saying this now and I will say it again, I thought my eating disorder was a phase. I honestly believed that I would grow out of it in a year or so. This 'phase' took fifteen years to even begin to start getting rid of. Besides the physical things, trying to recover in a culture where fasting, detoxing, keto, paleo, etc. are being painted over our eyes. I have even seen companies challenge people to fasting competitions. The sick part of me wants to do this and just blow their minds. I won't though. For the people trying to detox, I am really sorry your organs don't work. Y'all understand that, right? Our kidneys, liver, spleen, etc. are designed to eliminate things from our bodies. You have a built-in detox system. Whatever you are doing is not helping your organs. The keto diet scares me the most. As anyone with an eating disorder knows, ketosis is that thing we are happy to know we are going through. BECAUSE YOUR BODY IS EATING ITSELF. That shit is so dangerous, it's like pre-death symptoms. If anyone starts to get any sort of pineapple, rubbing alcohol sensation in their mouth - please, please, please get help.

There is a story by Hans Christian Andersen that I have always loved about the Snow Queen. In the story there is a brother and sister and a goblin with a mirror that shows the ugliness in the world. Everyone in the town wants to look through the mirror. They even fly up into the air to look at the angels through the mirror. The mirror shatters and shards fall into the brother's eye, causing his perception of reality to be off. That's always how I have felt. Like the Snow Queen's goblin has placed shards of mirror in my eye and I can't see correctly. It is not the rabbit hole that I ventured into. It is a frozen, shivering world of warped perceptions. My eyes only saw with a mirror that allows me to see myself as too much; too fat, taking up too much space. On the rare occasions I did see myself shrinking, it was not enough. I needed to disappear faster. Each time I lost weight, it was not enough, it was proof that I could push myself even farther. I was the child held captive by the queen and goblin in one. I placed the broken mirror into my own eyes with no plan on how to remove it.

Save As Draft

IN THE PAST WEEK, I have been roofied, my brother's mental health has become the worst it's ever been, and I lost my job. I feel so heavy from the tears not cried. As if each tear is weighing me down. I have cries in me that would create the ocean in Wonderland.

So many things have gone through my mind. Why do these things happen? What else is coming? How do I bounce back from any of this? I have no answers, only more concern and sadness.

If only I hadn't gone with those people; I wouldn't have been roofied. If only my brother could find happiness.

I feel like I'm a good person. I don't know how so much bad can happen in such a short amount of time. I don't know what else I have to do. How much more praying? How much more selflessness needs to happen before things start to get better for me? I don't know what I have to do; but God, I am trying.

Me. Too.

IN THE WAKE OF this #metoo craze, I have reflected on how fingers are pointed only at the male population when this is so not a male-against-female issue. Unwanted sexual advances come in all shapes and sizes from all shapes, sizes, and genders of people; and I think a lot of the time, the most widely accepted sexual harasser is ourselves.

I will speak to my own experiences, taking a long hard look at all the times I have either accepted or fed into my own sexual harassment. How many times have I smiled or winked at someone because I saw they were looking at me? Even if I wasn't attracted to them in any way, I wanted to appear pleasing to them. How many times have I kissed, made out with, crawled into bed with someone willingly that I didn't necessarily want to be doing those things with? If asked what it is about that person I like or find attractive, I would come up with nothing. How many times have I made myself up as much as possible for a job interview or to go to work? Sex sells, and I have fallen right down that rabbit hole time and time again to get that job or those extra tips. I'm sure there are countless other times I have been an object at my own hand; and for this, I take full responsibility and apologize to myself.

Then of course, there are the outside forces. These people are: male, female, old, young, strangers, friends, family, homeless, wealthy. There is no demographic that sexual harassment does not hit. It is not an issue for just one group of people. It is everyone. People against each other. So how do we rise up against this? I think we start by telling our stories. We face this head on and recognize how not alone we are in all this. We should not be ashamed, and we should not be cast down for speaking our truth. I have had a hard time with my #metoo because well, I thought it just wasn't anyone's fucking business. Then, as I saw it grow, I realized just how important it was for us, all of us, to speak up:

- To the neighbors/friend who forced me into 'play time', I say me too.
- To the boy who lured me outside, I say me too.
- To the fiancé who told me he didn't believe in spousal abuse because it was a contract to be his whenever, I say me too.
- To the countless people who invited me places just to get me drunk and take advantage of it. I am still having a hard time with this idea still, I say me too.
- To the family member who got too close, I say me too.

- To the boy who roofied me and then got handsy and still pulls my hair and wraps his hand around my neck, I say me too.
- To the people who didn't believe the last story, I say me too.
- To everyone who has ever controlled me, I say me too.
- To those who have grabbed, catcalled, sent or shown me images I didn't ask for, I say me too.
- To the ones who think being a female is easier and that we aren't as smart or powerful or worthy, I cry me too.
- To the people who cannot use their voice yet and speak up about their stories, I roar me too.

Power Up

I'M GOING TO TRY doing that "Thirty Days of Thankfulness" thing this year. I had a hard time thinking of what to start the month out with when there is so much to be thankful for. In the midst of all the negativity around, predominantly male actions, I wanted to take this first day and thank some of the men in my life:

My dad, who in the past twenty-four hours has taught me how to drive/operate a tractor, install a door, and relearn how to use a saw/drill.

Jim, for originally teaching me how to use power tools and how living organically is very important.

Myron, for being my sounding board through academics and pushing me in ways I needed to be pushed.

Craig, for being my stage dad and a wealth of knowledge and inspiration always.

Chris, for being the most supportive person. You saw me when I didn't see me.

Noah, for being the cutest boy to ever hold my hand and heart. I hope you never let go[6].

Mike, for being the bravest person I have ever met.

All of these men have, and continue, to inspire me and build me up with their actions, their words, their love, and the way they live their lives. I am so lucky to have such amazing men in my life. Sometimes, in all the pain and suffering, it is hard to remember the good. These are some of my good people. I think it's especially important that I put out into the universe my good people, to balance out revisiting some old wounds. In order to move on, grow, live, and breathe for one more day, we always need to look for the good people who show up for us. They are out there. If there is good in me and you, there is good in every single person. I do mean: Every. Single. Person. Has good in them. As human beings walking on this earth with other human beings, it is our job to be witness for the good that is in everyone. It is in all our hearts. We simply have to find it sometimes. Be the emotional explorers for others, as long as it does not come at our own expense.

However, being good does not mean well-behaved. I have spent too much of my life thinking that 'being good' and 'doing good' were the same. We label 'being good' with things like how we eat, or our etiquette, how we dress, or how loud we are, or how much space we take up. Good is not defined by how many salads you eat, if you eat that salad with the 'right' fork, look like everyone else, talk with your meek voice only, or shrink to make others comfortable. I am here to tell you, and I am afraid no one ever has or at

---

[6] *Noah is a toddler. No one get too excited.*

least no one has ever said it enough; eat to fill your soul and your body, eat with your damn hands if that is what fills you, dress in whatever makes you want to dance in the streets, yell/roar/shriek/rage whatever you have to do to be heard, and for heaven's sake, please take up all the room you desire. You deserve it. I will repeat this again. You deserve to take up all the space your heart desires. Do not make yourself small so that other people feel comfortable. Do not be small to try and make other people happy. You were not meant to shrink down, and you do not have the power to make other people feel any type of way. We are only given endless power as long as we focus it on ourselves. I am learning how to harness that power daily and I am most thankful for that.

Adventures in Forgiveness

HE CAME AFTER ME while I was taking care of my grandmother at the end of her life, in her house. That one particular day changed everything.

When I told my mom, her first reaction was that she was afraid something like this would happen eventually because he has always considered himself a lady's man. Wait... you suspected this was going to happen?! No one put anything in place to prevent this?! Her next thought was that she didn't know what to do, no more than I did. We didn't want to pull apart the family.

I didn't see him very often after that. Every day though, for a while, I would live in terror of him showing up. When he did, I would hide, pretend I wasn't there so I didn't have to be around him. Years have passed, and I still panic when I see car lights in the dark because I am afraid someone has gotten drunk enough, and mad enough, and lustful enough to come for me.

Recently, he suffered an awful health scare and was in the hospital for a long-winded stay. We thought he wasn't going to make it. Visiting him was the first time I had seen him since the incident. I held his hand and sat with him and wasn't sure what to think about this man's life ending.

Well, he made it out of the woods and while it isn't often, he does stop by. Yesterday he gave me a hug and a kiss on the head. Some moments I am fine being around him, others I get triggered, and sometimes both things happen. I have realized though that sometimes being an adult is forgiving people for the unforgivable. How, when, who, and if we forgive these people is up to each of us alone. I do think that not forgiving keeps us, not the other person, trapped in our own emotions. With forgiveness, we give ourselves the opportunity to grow, love, grieve, and move past the things that seem impassable[7].

This does not mean we forget and act like everything is fine. Do not forget the things that have dragged you down. In some way, the lessons you learn from these experiences will serve you. You have to learn from them though, otherwise they will only hurt you. How often have we all seen on a concrete sidewalk grass, moss, or even a tree growing in the cracks? Something growing where there shouldn't be growth at all. Use your cracks. Grow! Live! Overcome!

---

[7] *You don't actually ever have to accept an apology or let someone know you forgive them. Sometimes people need to learn the price of their actions by not being forgiven. Just don't let it hurt yourself.*

On The Eve of Thankfulness

EVERY YEAR, NOVEMBER seems to kick off the season of thanks, giving, love, good spirits. We have all looked at the calendar, quickly shoved the costumes and candy aside, and took a moment to breathe in gratefulness. I am sure there are those people who are just putting up a good show. Their social media accounts are overflowing with thoughts of thanks. When in reality, they are still their grumpy selves. Others really have taken that breath of thanks and are making the most out of the last two months in the year.

Whichever kind of person you are, I think that for everyone, it is okay to not feel overwhelmed with thankfulness on Thanksgiving. We have spent the day, week, hours, whatever planning, and prepping, and buying, and preening, and hoping for a joyous holiday. Every year, I do the same thing. I help make food, I find a great new outfit (because everyone needs the right outfit for battle), and I amp myself up. It is these expectations that we put on ourselves and our families that really cause the holiday to... well, suck.

For a person with an eating disorder, Thanksgiving is a scary time. It is a food-centered holiday and everyone is expected to eat too much all at once and not eat for the rest of the day. This day is terrifying, this day is the day that sets people back. All year, hard work has been done to achieve eating habits that work with our bodies. Then, Thanksgiving comes along. For me, so many things come up during this holiday. Do I eat breakfast? When do I eat breakfast? If we are eating at 2pm, does that count as lunch and dinner? Is my plate too full? Is my plate not full enough? Who thought turnips were a good idea? All of this, all day. I have discovered many times over, that I actually don't like most Thanksgiving foods: stuffing, turnips, sweet potatoes (especially with marshmallows), butternut squash that has been brown sugared. I really don't enjoy it. My eating disorder loves it. When there are foods I don't like, I have a good reason to eat less. When there is a giant party, no one will wonder where I am if I disappear into the crowd and into the bathroom for an hour. No one will wonder why I'm not eating dessert if I say I ate too much before. Thanksgiving made my eating disorder sing. So how do I navigate it now? In a family, who questions whether it even existed at all? In a house where someone proclaims we need to stop buying food because there is too much in the house. This day brings up more questions than I have answers.

In sharing this, I want everyone to remember that if today, if tomorrow, if any holiday is hard, you are not alone. For every moment of holiday traffic, every toxic relative, bad food, uncomfortable sweaters and situations; I am right there with you. To the people who do have warm houses and warm hearts to go to, and this day is fun; rejoice in it. Families are chaotic and wonderful. Enjoy the love chaos. Celebrate it, and maybe send some of that love our way.

And Yes, To Life

When I was about fifteen years of age, my entire summer was dedicated to an Outpatient Eating Disorder Treatment. I remember sitting in that building, surrounded by women about a decade older than I was, and thinking I didn't want to still have this eating disorder when I was their age. You see, in my head, this was simply a phase. Something that would pass me because I had grown out of it like butterfly clips, or dying my hair, or glitter (ok, I haven't grown out of the last two things yet)[8]. It never occurred to me that my eating disorder would last.

That's the thing though. It is MY eating disorder. In a world where so much has been taken from me or isn't mine, this one thing was all mine. Now, I am thirty and my eating disorder has finally turned into my eating disorder recovery. It is the one thing I have that is mine still, because the choice to recover comes only from one person - YOU. I also have discovered the beautiful art of asking for help.

---

[8] *Also, someone please make butterfly clips cool again. I'm ready.*

I spent almost a year in Tennessee doing residential treatment for my eating disorder and PTSD. It was in the smallest town known to man with its giant bugs and laughable winters, and it was there that I learned how to be a person again. I went in kicking and screaming, dreading having to spend all my time with twenty other women at all times. I was convinced I could not get along with people of my same gender and apparently, this was the really big problem for me - not the fact that I had made such a mess of things that I had to be in treatment in the first place. It turns out, I knew very little about myself. Those women ended up being the best and most important sources of support I have ever met. Someone was always there to talk, open a window, get water, or simply hold space for you. To this day, years later, with the grace of social media powers, I am still in contact with all of them and I am so wonderfully blessed.

I am also blessed that gone are the days where my entire life is consumed by thoughts of weight, food, numbers, exercise. I no longer wake up from dreams where all I am doing was eating, terrified I had actually eaten in real life. I am no longer passing out against the side of a building or in bathrooms on a weekly basis. I am no longer refusing social interaction for fear that food may be involved. Do I still struggle? Yes, absolutely. 100%. There are times when my brain tries to slide me back into behaviors. It was comfortable, and it was all mine. The difference is that I have hard moments now, not a hard life. While I am finally learning what I like doing, and where my passions and hobbies lie, I know I am learning these things as the fullest most authentic version of me that I have ever been. There is so much to learn, and I am so glad I am sticking around to learn it.

Surrender, Eventually

YEARS AGO, I FOUND a church I actually connected with. Well, let's go back. When I was taking care of my grandmother full-time, I became the third generation in my family to join the church in that town. This church is basically a family heirloom. Something was missing though. I loved the minister; the old white ladies were all adorable and everything. It just wasn't it though.

Then I went down south. Yes, I know. Who can believe that in the south, someone may actually find a church they like?! I did. I loved it, didn't even mind that it was more than an hour. I can still see the prayer leaders, still smell the building, could still point out the fire escape that was a little too close to the children's classroom where we use to smoke. I loved going, looked forward to it even, which is very surprising for me.

You see, I grew up thinking church was that white New England church that is on every town green. They are not decorated, there are choir robes, pews, organs, hymnals. These were the churches I was told church was. I hated Sunday school, hated getting dressed up, hated memorizing prayers. I did, for a number of years, ask for a cross necklace but as it turns out, decorating yourself is just as frowned upon as decorating your church.

I had given up on church. I had not, however, given up on God. And boy, had God not given up on me. Every single moment that my brother and I take a breath, we are living proof that God has not given up on us. Even when we had given up on ourselves many times over. Maybe I had given up on God a little. I don't think it is fair to say I have control issues, addiction issues, relationship issues of every kind and also say you love God completely. All those things are the things used in place of God. To fill the God-sized hole with everything except God. They also make God easier to find once you realize those things are not serving you. It's easy to crawl on dirty hands and knees to finally realize that you and your maladaptive coping skills look nothing like God. They are, however, a road map to finding your higher power. The map is not easy to read, sometimes it leads you so far away, and you forget God is an option. God, the door knob, love, whatever you call your higher power, is always an option. There is always a way back.

Today, after many months of thinking I should go, I walked into the doors of a new church. It was not white, it was not full of old white ladies, and it did not have pews or hymnals. It just had people. Loving, amazing, beautiful people. Many of them noticed the newcomer and didn't just shake my hand, but talked to me, got to know me, showed me around. Wow, was this a different experience! As we settled down for worship, it was full of music led by a band! A fucking band! Can you believe some churches have bands!? They were great, and people sang, and then we got to prayers and the message of the day (I don't feel right calling it sermon because we were being invited into the words, not talked at). Then after, more people talked to me! I left that place feeling so much. Confused as to why they people were so nice (I don't trust nice people all that much), elated, lifted, like I had new eyes to the world. I have so many questions and the same real people who talked to me have reached out and guided me to who best can help.

Of course, now my biggest worry is how to approach my questions? How do I be me and still be good enough for this community? Can I trust my new mentor to hear my stories and not decide that I am beyond help? Can I be this eating disordered, mentally struggling, swearing, sex-having human being and still get right with God? If I can get right with myself, God can probably get right with me too. Higher powers really like to show off sometimes.

This is what the let go and let God thing is, isn't it? Forgiving yourself because your higher power already has. Learning I do not have the control, because I fuck it up beyond all hope when I try that. Ya'll, I think I have finally got it. God bless the slow learner, and I am so blessed.

.... The journey starts now.

Physical Bodies

I WAS GOING TO talk about this last night, however, I think I needed some time to think about it. I was talking to one of my friends (using the word "friend" casually here) and explaining to him that if we were to be talking in the same room right at that moment instead of texting, there would be no cuddling. I went on to explain that there would be no cuddling because I am giving up physical relationships with everyone. There were questions and I did not seem to answer them to his liking. He told me that in giving up physical relationships, I was going to cause mistrust in people, get in my own way, and ruin a potentially good thing with someone. He then told me very unexpectedly (or maybe not) that he had to go to sleep and I have not heard from him since. This is not unusual since I really only hear from him when he is lonely and begging for attention. Last night was no different. He was lonely, he wanted female attention, he got shut down and was shocked when I wasn't playing along.

But now I have questions; *why* is my decision of what I do with my body in relation to anyone else's allowed to be such an open discussion? Why is my decision to not have physical relations supposedly going to ruin my chances of having a good relationship? Why would that cause mistrust? Wouldn't the idea of me sleeping with more people rather than no people cause that? Does he realize his response is the exact reason I am doing this in the first place?

I have chosen to no longer use physical contact as a way to connect with people. Or rather, for a way for people to connect with me. I have never found any intimacy in sleeping with someone. Mostly, it just feels like a chore or a duty. I understand that lots of people connect through physical touch and so I go along with it. Unlike what seems to be a common trend amongst intimacy, I find intimacy way more of a mental thing. That in order to feel loved and worthy, people need to feel attractive and wanted and they prove this in physical acts. I no longer will be participating in this, and I hope to find that I will have deeper emotional connections to the people in my life.

At least with the ones who stick around knowing I will not jump into bed with them.

An Unpopular Opinion - An Addendum

I HAVE UNCONVENTIONAL FEELINGS about the #MeToo movement; and not for the reasons most people would assume. For me, this movement that is supposed to bring people together and give woman a voice, actually causes me to feel more alone. I am angry every time I see a new article pop up about another allegation. Angry at the woman for pointing fingers at yet another famous person, angry at the female celebrities who are speaking up and claiming they will tell my story, angry at the fact that somehow this is a Hollywood-centric fad.

I am angry at these women because the more of them that speak up, the further away we seem to get from stories of true assault. Now it seems that everyone gets to 'cry wolf' when they are uncomfortable in a situation. Part of being an adult human being is the great gift of being in charge of a lot of things, including our own comfort. *We* are responsible for our own comfort. When we hand that over to someone else and then act surprised when they cross a line, I don't think it's a subject for newspapers. That was a choice that was made. Speak up instead. The idea that everyone needs to be reading body language to make sure someone is 'into it' is a great idea. It is also a pipe dream. In the throes of lust, the only person anyone is paying attention to is themselves. I have come to know that it really doesn't matter so much if you act like an enthusiastic porn star or lay there staring in space. Someone will mash their sweaty body against yours and will say how amazing that was, and then ask if you had fun. If it's a touch or a glance, they will assume you are also into it unless you say something or move away. Even then, they may decide you are playing 'hard to get'. I am also angry because if someone saying something uncomfortable to these women is the worst thing that has ever happened to them, and it must be since it makes the news, we are worlds away in our experiences and that right there is the isolation factor. I have never lived in a world where words were the worst thing done to me. The words didn't help the situation and certainly made a situation worse a lot of the time. However, the words were a small part of the problem. I was not born into it, I did not grow up in it, and I do not live there now. This, more than anything, causes me to feel more alone due to this movement.

To the movement makers who are boasting that they will tell my story: please don't. Having things taken from me that I try and claim as my own is the problem. Please do not help that continue. My story belongs to me. I will share, or not share, with whomever I like in whatever time frame I wish. It is my choice, though. It does not belong to you.

I am afraid that this overzealous, backed-by-Hollywood movement is going to cause the world to burn down a little. If a manhunt, in a literal sense, is to be started, where does it stop? In what corners of our world do we not look into to try and find more men (because let's face it, this thing has been made only about what men are doing) who are making women uncomfortable? If that happens, if every single male has to be ridden from their jobs every time a female is made uncomfortable, there will be nothing left. We need to keep men around. They think differently than women, which is not a bad thing. There are so many good, forward-thinking people in this world. The thing is though, they are still just people. All of them, human beings: flawed, messy, emotional, damaged, loving human beings. If we can't forgive other people for not being perfect, for letting us down, for not meeting the ideal we thought they should meet, and if we don't express clearly these things or cry foul play when our needs are not met (that's an inward thing by the way; meet your own needs, don't expect someone else to do it) how are we ever going to learn how to forgive ourselves?

Why We Tell the Story

LAST WEEK, WHEN I attended church, prayers were sent out to a young woman who was in the hospital because of a drug overdose. I asked someone in the congregation to please connect me with her family as I felt I could give them some hope. The week passed, and I heard nothing. Today in church, I finally connected with her grandmother, and let me tell you, I am so glad we waited and were able to have the conversation we did in person.

I sat with the older woman and told her to look at me; see that I am a living, breathing person in front of her right now. That I am only able to be any of those things because I was saved in the same hospital her granddaughter was in. A year and a half ago, I overdosed, I was in a coma, my heart rate and blood pressure dropped so low that they really figured I was going to die. I didn't. I am here, I am saved. I tried to die and that small voice inside of me waited until it was the only thing left in my body. It's time to yell, 'My story isn't done! I have more to do!' had come. I am so glad it did. Though the days following that coma are foggy, and my family had to experience watching me circle the drain and I wasn't there mentally to bear witness, I showed up for myself. I lived.

There were tears, hugs, and a lot of I love yous. I imparted on her that nothing will change unless her granddaughter wanted it, that she had to keep everything simple right now, and this was in no way the family's fault. I gave her my number and told her that she and the rest of her family could reach out.

Addiction, of any kind, is a very isolating thing. I was addicted to my own anger, addicted to suffering and sadness. I did not survive just to keep my story to myself. I cannot change the things I put my family through. I wasn't even really there. I do have the power now to help other families. I, in fact, do not have the right to not help them. I did not go through things and let my family go through things just to come out the other end and keep quiet when a situation comes up where I may be able to help. I think AA has that part just right. You stay in recovery by helping other people. I will continue to bring my experience, strength, and hope to those who need it. I was given a do-over, a chance to try again. May my life now be testament to overcoming the internal monster.

Another Unpopular Opinion

IT SEEMS THAT just about every day, someone is complaining about how Narcan is free and insulin and chemo are still expensive. Insulin and chemo are what I consider treatment drugs. They are used to treat a disease. At least in the case of chemo, you stop at some point and your disease may be gone.

Narcan is used when the other option is death. Not in a few weeks, months, years, but in the moment, now. Death will happen right then. So, let's say they are given Narcan, shipped off to the hospital in an ambulance, and not only is their heart working again, but they realized someone decided they were worth saving. Maybe this gets them on the road to treatment. That road ahead will require residential stays, outpatient treatments, therapy, and most likely psych meds. On top of the hospital stay, and ambulance ride that got them to this point. That one free hit of Narcan may be the only free thing they receive while healing.

If this is really about comparing cancer to addiction, let me pipe in my very unpopular opinion for a moment.

Cancer can be cured; with surgery, meds, diet, whatever you want to do. It can be cured. A cancer patient can go on to live a full life still. The other side, of course, is that they don't beat cancer and they die, usually in a morphine cloud (irony) and off they go. Addiction has no cure. No amount of anything is going to ever stop the addict from having it in the back of their mind that they could pick up again. They have to learn to fight with themselves every day. Sometimes they die too, and it is sudden and awful and probably not in a great environment.

I also do not believe it is fair to compare the two monsters. It puts a mental disease up against a physical one. They are so different, and both destroy so many lives. The lives that are taken, and the lives that are left to grieve. It is unfair to say at any point that funding for one disease should be taken and used for the other. No life is worth more than another. No Life. Is Worth. More. Than. Another. Ever.

The big differences to me are that I have never seen an addict post on social media 'today is the day I found out I had cancer x number of years ago'. I have never heard an addict that has chosen to make a different choice, use their addiction as an excuse. I have never seen or heard of someone choosing to label themselves as an addict because it runs in their family, so they decide to remove parts of themselves as a safety measure. Often, there are a lot of clean and sober people walking around on this earth and we never know. People who have had cancer are pretty quick to tell you that about themselves.

Cancer is awful, terrible, and it ruins lives. So is addiction. If measures can be taken to help alleviate an awful, terrible, life-ruining thing and it's free, why are we debating it's worth? Why are we debating if any life is worth more than another? There is nothing except death that you can't come back from. People with addictions and with cancer know this so well because *they have looked death in the face*. For me, I think how you choose to handle that type of situation speaks volumes. Once a life has seen revival, there can be a grace and a selflessness that comes with knowing, for sure, that we are not permanent.

My bet is on the addict being that person. Every. Time.

Mind and Body

ONE OF THE MANY, many, many (soooo many) things they don't tell you about having an eating disorder is the parts that never leave you. I will have health problems forever and I will learn to live with that. There is something I have a hard time with still: being sick.

No one likes being sick. I get that. When you have a brain that expects perfection, being sick is a worst-case scenario. When I was younger, I would just suck it up during times I really should have not been sucking it up. I once had Swine Flu and still worked over half a day, even though I wasn't sure I could stand. I also once pushed myself to continue my 8am-10pm college routine even though I had a fever of 104. I was not going to let being sick get in my way, no matter what.

Now, I thankfully allow myself to rest and I try hard not to expose anyone to my germs when I am sick. The first thing that happens in my head is that I get mad at myself. If I am sick and unable to perform at my best, I feel ineffective and useless and I get angry that I am sick. If the illness lasts long enough this turns into depression and that can linger long after the illness is over. I have caught myself faking illness for days after I feel better, so I can justify doing nothing.

The most lingering thing, though, is of course about my weight. When truly sick, I find it hard to eat anything, so I force toast, crackers, soup. This diet, along with my body fighting an illness, usually causes a change in my body. One I am quick to notice and quick to hold on to. I see weight loss and my brain goes to, 'hey, we can keep this up' and 'we can do better'.

I am there now. I was sick for three weeks with the virus from Hell[9] which caused weight loss, and though I am feeling better, my mind is not. I have found myself being disgusted by most food. The only thing I have been able to really get myself to eat is peanut butter and jelly. I have somehow resorted to kid food and almost refuse anything else.

I will say that today was still a win. I went out to lunch after church with some friends. While I did not eat a lot, I did try and branched out from the foods I have stuck with the past month. There is hope somewhere in me. I just have to push to find the parts of me that want to be better.

---

[9] *I think every virus I get is at least the plague. I love dramatics.*

For Today and Every Day

ONE THING IN MY life that I have learned is that it is far easier to walk away than it is to stay and love someone. Love comes with hard work, hard choices, and even harder, scarier vulnerability. People are messy - love them anyway. People will disappoint you, not live up to your expectations, or whatever ideals Hollywood and books have put in our heads - love them anyway. People will make mistakes, they will hurt you - love them anyway. People won't always understand you - love them anyway. Everyone was perfectly made on this earth, trying to fill the God-sized hole that is within them. There will be stumbling, hard times, things we don't understand because "I would never do that" - love them anyway. Most importantly, you are also all of these things; imperfect, struggling, disappointing, mistake making, hurtful and full of hurt - love yourself anyway. If on any day you can't, come sit by me, we will figure out how together. We are all so loved and so worth the space we take up. Please take up some space with me. I love you, keep going.

Enough

I RECENTLY HAD to cut ties with someone. After a few months of knowing them, it had become clear that they were not in the right headspace to be filling up space in my life. I look for the best in people and remind myself that everyone is doing their own version of best. It comes off as harsh, and I also know it is true; sometimes a person's best is not good enough to fit in your life.

I am at a place where I try every day to be open, honest, supportive, and live wholeheartedly. I give so much of myself to other people. I encourage them, I communicate to the best of my abilities in the moment, I do what I can to keep them comfortable and happy. Just as someone's best may not be a good fit for me, I know that my best may not be a good fit for someone else. A person can try every day to support another, go the extra mile for them, hold space, listen to how they express and receive love and go out and do those things. Still, it may not be enough, it may not be what they need.

For this particular person, I feel that they have not yet discovered self-love. I find that when this is the case, no one will ever be enough. You can not do enough or be enough for a person who has not learned how to love themselves. They hope to find the love they need in external things. They hope that the right amount of people, food, booze, laughter, whatever will finally fill the void they are feeling. That God-sized hole is huge in those who are seeking outward. If someone has not yet discovered that everything they need is already inside of them, nothing will ever be enough.

I have done my best to not let my anger best me while I am separating. A lot of hurtful things were said and done. I am learning to not be afraid of anger, so what that means for me is letting myself feel it. Where I use to take anger out on myself, I now work to recognize it, accept it, and feel it so I am able to move forward. It does no good to hurt myself because I am angry at another person or situation. I feel angry and I feel sad. I know I am not responsible for someone else's journey. I am more than willing to support them along the way. I am not willing to put myself in the path of their journey when they are not even ready to begin it.

I may have not been enough for one particular person, but I am enough for myself. Because of this, I can now see that if someone is lacking in their own self-love to the point that it is hurting me, I am able to walk away. I hope each time I do this I am able to do it gently for both of us. When people in my life cannot see me as a person but a way to save them, I know we need to go our separate ways. I will not lose myself, I will not give up the enough that I am for me in order to try and be enough for someone else.

Things Lost and Found In the Fire

FIRE IS A FUNNY THING. It is destructive, and given enough of the right things, it will take down everything in its path. Fire can also be a blessing, as it can be used to cleanse the earth. When humans first arrived, they discovered fire as a way to keep warm and it solidified their contributions to the earth's history.

I think that people are fires. They come in and destroy with their bad actions and judgmental words. They take down everything in their path for the sake of their own agenda. Given enough fuel, they will take down walls, buildings, entire empires, a life.

Let them. That is not to say willingly walk into a fire - we all know that outcome.[10] Don't keep people around who are hurting you. I believe that two people are always brought together because they have lessons to teach each other. Even if that person is the destructive kind of fire. Maybe they were put on your path because for whatever

---

[10] *Unless you have been trained to walk on hot coals. In which case, please call me. I want to learn.*

reason, the overgrowth of your life needed to be cleansed. Find the warmth. If you feel stripped away of your roots, know that even after a terrible fire, not all is lost. For there, under the ashes, new life begins.

No one can take away your strong sense of self love and purpose. Grow with what has felt like a damaging encounter. Plant your roots so well that no one can destroy them. Light your own fire. Be the warm kind, the cleansing kind, the kind that starts new life.

In my own journey, I have been met with many destructive fires. In fact, I was created by a destructive fire. While I feel anger and sadness and all those things we like to label 'bad emotions,' it has also helped me. In being torn down, I have learned how to find new life, and maybe this has let me go down a different road I never would have even thought to travel. I have also learned that any validation or love or anything I need, I can give to myself. I am the fire.

I recognize that I have enough fuel to give out light and warmth to others. I have the ability to help level what is weighing them down in order to find their roots. I hope for all of you that you are able to find your fire and use it for light and warmth and use it to start over when needed.

Growing Pains

THIS MORNING, I AM living my best life. I woke up next to my boyfriend, we went out to breakfast, and now we are in the same room, working on different things. I get to hear his soul feeling songwriting as I write this. I get to look over and smile at him as we each work on our own things. Right now, this moment, I feel like everything in my life has led me to right here. The simple, relaxed co-existing with someone when there is no need to put aside other things. This morning has been so perfect and so needed.

The past few weeks have been hell for us. We are both working way more than any human should be working, plus he's moving. Life has been getting the better of us.

The worst part of it by far was the lack of appetite. Nothing appealed to me no matter what my sweet boyfriend put in front of me. This, of course, sparked my eating disorder and I have since been struggling with food. Every time I try to eat, I go in to a panic that makes me unable to move. I have set myself on living off black coffee, cigs, and diet coke. This does NOT help with the long work days and exhaustion and stress and anxiety. My brain flips and becomes a monster. I have Jekyll and Hyde living in my mind. My capacity to be mean and awful and paranoid astounds me. Where I was calm and soothing, I have no patience and where I was believing in the best of people, I jump to the worst conclusions based off nothing.

This seeped into my relationship and made it hard to even convince myself that spending anytime with boyfriend was something I needed or wanted. We are both stressed and tired and being pulled apart. Instead of remembering that together we can be the one still point in the universe, we tried to dig up problems where none existed.

Today, I have been given a gift. Life has cried out 'this is important!' This person, this relationship, these emotions. Feel it all, lean in to it. In a situation that could have broken us, I feel closer and more connected to my boyfriend. I had my fears of the worst. Today, I have only joy.

Birthday Lights

THIS WEEK IS my birthday. Not the date that it says on my birth certificate but the date, in which, I finally emerged from my own self-constructed womb and entered the world. I will be two. Before that, I was not so safely hiding inside of fear, doubt, anger, self-loathing, unworthiness, and shame. This all trapped me so tightly that I used my umbilical cord to snuff myself out. It just looked like over a hundred prescription medications, so I was confused.

I passed out on my parents' living room floor while I was about to go to work. That somewhere made sense in my oxygen-starved brain to get in a car and try and do any job because 'Hey. I'm fine.'[11] Four days later, I woke up from a coma. I talked to a lot of people, I don't remember, I apparently bought a lot of shoes online, I don't remember. I do remember the ICU nurses encouraging me while my mom propped me up as I walked around the nurses' station in order to get strength back. They let me pick my own

---

[11] *Please, if you have taken any pills, any drugs, done any drinking, don't try and drive a car. Please don't.*

Pandora station (The Civil Wars) and had the greatest smiles. My mom later sent them a care package as a thank you.

I then spent a week in a psych ward. I paced up and down the hallways like a caged animal, and fell heavily into my eating disorder. I tried to convince them many times to let me go. They, of course, didn't. One of the med techs took an interest in me; not as a person, but as an interesting case study since my overdose was some combination of PTSD/DID and I did not remember trying to kill myself, let alone feeling suicidal.

When I finally did get turned out into the world, it was the day of a family party. I was about to be surrounded by people my mom has known since kindergarten and therefore are better family than some of our biological family. That sounds exactly like birth to me, you enter the world and are immediately surrounded by your tribe. The party was hard, and I felt in a daze. It was a lot to go from psych ward bubble to music and loud talking and bright colors and food that wasn't glowing yellowish-gray.

In time I began to relearn things, adjust, figure out where a change needed to be. I can't say that I immediately had this feeling of, 'this is my second chance and I am going to kill it (bad joke?).' I felt lost and like I had no idea what I was doing, and things were hard, and I was still sad, and my family was upset and since 'I wasn't really there in that ICU room, I couldn't know what it was like'. I still struggled. I still struggle. The crawl out of the mud is long and hard. I had times where I cried so hard, I threw up. I had times where I thought I was succeeding, and my family didn't, and I wanted to remind them that I was just born but that would probably be painful for them.

Now, going on two years later, I have to laugh all the time. Life is still hard, and life is also beautiful. The things I thought were impossible were not. I didn't know that two years after my birth, I would have a job, friends, and partner that I love. I didn't know that the things I would have to 'complain' about are everyday things. That feels wonderful. Boring is pretty nice when I was born out of chaos.

Tonight, I was sitting outside with the cats watching the first fireflies of the season come to my yard. I was reminded of the children's book *The Very Lonely Firefly*. I realized that book is not for children. It is a tale of a single firefly that is lonely and looks for other fireflies by flashing its light. It takes a really long time and the firefly feels sad and ready to give up. Of course, the firefly finds the other fireflies and the very last page is decked out with a whole bunch of actual real flashing lights made to look like fireflies. It's magic. Seriously, go find this book.

Life and recovery are so like that. You have to create your own light. You have to struggle, and feel sad, and be ready to give up and *still* create your own light. Do this long enough and hard enough, you will find your tribe of firefly people.

Flicker on my friends, and try not to get trapped in a jar!

The Ocean, In Drops

FOR WHATEVER REASON, I have been thinking about cruises recently - and not because I have any desire to find myself on a ship. The idea of a cruise actually sounds terrible to me. Being stuck on a giant boat in a giant body of water to fake places with a ton of people and expensive stores. Sure, you can get off the boat and take day trips, but eventually it is back to the giant floating department store with its excessive amounts of food and booze to keep you forgetting that you are, in fact, on a boat.

The concept of a cruise actually sounds a lot like life to me. We are floating along and act like we have everything we need right at our fingertips. As if the people we are floating along with came along by accident and yes, we just LOVE all the cute stores and public pools and booze and thousands of Instagram moments.

Maybe we start our lives on a cruise ship. We make stops, get out, explore, come back to the comfort of what we know. The things picked out for us because we are born into them. The people that get on and off during the voyage are not there on accident. Each and every one of them put in our path for a reason. Along the way, we sedate ourselves with food and booze and parties. Because in some small way, we know we are just stuck on a boat.

It's scary to realize you are surrounded by water, the unknown on every side. We don't go out too far because we are afraid. We would rather stick to what we know. We do not want to drown or get swept away. We like to stay comfortable. Even if it isn't comfortable at all, just what we are use to.

Here is the good news! We are all made up of tiny oceans. We do not have to be afraid to venture out into the unknown because it already is a part of us. We are frightened because it is our inner ocean swelling up to meet the greater ocean that made us. Sometimes it may be cold, dark, full of things we have never imagined. Humans float, we do not want to drown. People know how to swim to far shores and venture into the great unknown. This is why we feel calm when it rains, why we have pulls to be near a beach or a lake. We WANT to go back to the water we are made of.

I was talking with someone last night about how one of their very first memories is a Mr. Rogers song about not being afraid in the bathtub. I had never heard this song before and looked it up:

You can never go down
Can never go down
Can never go down the drain.
You can never go down
Can never go down
Can never go down the drain.

You're bigger than the water,
You're bigger than the soap,
You're much bigger than all the bubbles
And bigger than your telescope, so you see...
You can never go down
Can never go down
Can never go down the drain.
You can never go down
Can never go down
Can never go down the drain.
The rain my go down
But you can't go down
You're bigger than any bathroom drain.
You can never go down
Can never go down
Can never go down the drain.

These song lyrics hit me in ways I did not know a children's song could. We will survive being out of the water. It is already in us. It is in us though. Not everything we are. So, we can survive being in the water, we can survive being out of the water. We do not have to take the same path and go down. We do not fail. We are bigger than the water. We are bigger than anything. Remember that you have the ocean inside of you. Healing, changing, always moving oceans. The moon may cause the ocean to react, but the ocean caused the entire world to move. *You are bigger than even that!*

An Argument for Yoga

I HAD BEEN ALIVE on the planet for three whole years before I experienced my first sexual abuse. While I would love to say it stopped once my family moved states, it didn't. Up until recently, my life was in the sexual abuse cycle at the hands of over ten people. I knew all of them. Since this wasn't enough, I grew up in a house where drug and alcohol addiction were the norm. Somewhere in all of this, I figured the solution was an eating disorder. It robbed my life more than anything else could. I now have a strong aversion to exercise because it's hard to find a place for it when, after working in a restaurant for ten hours a day, I would run/do crunches/leg lifts/ anything for three hours each night. My PTSD also brought with it self-harm, depression, anxiety, and suicide attempts.

In 2014, I entered a residential treatment for nine months. It was nothing like they show in movies. We spent a lot of time exploring healing through Native American practices, equine therapy, energy healing, meditation, acupuncture, ropes courses, breath work, and yoga. This was not the first time I had ever experienced yoga. However, by the time it was reintroduced, I could not handle it. Focusing on breathing and being in my body felt like I was dying every time. It would cause me to dissociate. I was not ready. Still, I was told to do yoga. I was told to get on the mat and try. I did, and every time it was the same; panic, my body would shut down, and I would lose time. I thought that whatever anyone says they get out of yoga that is nice, relaxing, pure light, must be lies. I kept trying though. I'm not even sure why. It is the hardest work to ask someone who has only ever felt safe being out of their body and away from the world to try and stay present, stay in their bodies, and breathe in the entire universe. Given my past thought process that I needed to be perfect, yoga also didn't work for me because there was always the message of, 'do what is best for your body not what you think is right'. I really thought these yoga people were crazy to ask me to not be perfect.

Somewhere along the way, I had been able to ease myself into yoga and realize that, yes. Okay, I'm starting to understand what people are talking about. I also understand now that when you are in recovery from something, you tend to hate everything at first. This is actually a good thing. It is your old patterns screaming because they know they are about to be replaced. It also allowed me to notice some patterns in myself. That I was going to the psych ward every three months almost to the day. I made a radical choice to come off all the psych meds I had been given because I also noticed this pattern only started after I had started taking them. I was right, I did some metabolic testing and my body does not process psych meds in an appropriate way. They were amplifying symptoms I could deal with before. I have not entered a psych ward since[12].

A part of recovery is to share your experience, strength, and hope with other people. While my main goal is to learn more about myself through yoga, I want to eventually share it with others. Not just anyone either. I want to focus a lot on addiction and trauma-based yoga. Find the people who also started out thinking yoga was stupid and not helpful. Share my story and help them quiet the screaming of their maladaptive coping skills being replaced. I want the hard cases.

Right now, I have been given a hurdle. I have been told my brain has been injured to the point where my brain cells are dying at a faster rate than the average person. The good and bad news is that brains are like outer space. We still don't know a lot. There is no cure and there is also no certainty that I will have full blown dementia down the road. My limits look different than they did even a few weeks ago. I am currently unable to return to working at the group home I was in, I cannot be out in public for long periods of time, I get tired easily and usually have to nap. My memory and motor skills completely fail somedays. I spend some time being frustrated. I also spend a lot of time being grateful. I have, in a really dumb way, been given gift. I now *must* slow down. I have to wake up every day see where my limit is for the day. The things I do have more deliberate, and I now require that those around the same. I can not allow myself to put up with a to

---

[12] *I in no way endorse anyone stopping their meds at any reason. I was fucking lucky and fucking stupid.*

like I use to. I also no longer have space for the people in my life who are uncertain about being around. So much of this is hard. I loved my job however it came with a lot of stress. I may now get the chance to work for myself and in areas that fit with me better. I worry that I will not have someone who will be willing to put in the work to be in a romantic relationship with me long term. I was already a lot of work and my family members have their own significant others with degenerative diseases to worry about. I also know that I have set up for myself the most amazing tribe of people. I know that the last relationship I was in, was not the one I needed. No matter how much I tell myself it was different, I was still in a cycle of addiction and mental illness that belonged to a person who was not ready to recover.

I cannot say that I have met everything in my life with grace. Sometimes I really just want to have crying and yelling fits. This is actually a really good thing. I spent a lot of my life not allowing in any emotions. Humans are forever rks in progress. I am so ready to admit that I am human, ˙ct, and real.

Throwing Up In the Shower and Other Group Activities

I HAVE FOUND MYSELF up in the shower.... a lot ... again. I throw up in the shower because I am mad. This is how I have always been. I feel mad at a situation or person, so I throw up. I throw up, because along the way, I was taught that I should, 'remain calm', 'forgive', 'speak softly'. So instead of having a conversation about how I feel, I let my words pour out of me in vomit.

Throwing up is not a solo activity. I invite in every person and situation I have felt a thought about. I let them sit with me while I pour out every awful thing inside of me. I let the water wash over and out of me until I am empty of all the wrongdoings and sadness I feel from being human. I know I am empty when things start to slow down, colors get brighter. It's like being under water but instead of drowning, I am floating away from my feelings.

Sometimes I have invited other forms of self-harm to the party. I created works of art on my skin, see the water mix with my blood in some sad watercolor masterpiece. This is the opposite of trying to get empty. It's the feelings I want. Not only do I want to feel them, I want to see them. I want to see the work I have done and feel validated that what I feel is real.

I was never able to empty myself or bleed enough. So, I know I was doing the wrong things. I was doing the wrong things because I still didn't feel whole and sometimes outsiders felt scared. They told me to breathe, but I don't want to breathe. I don't want to let any more of the world in. I breathe anyway: I breathe and let air and space flow into the tiny cracks that surround the walls I have built. The air comes with light. The light creates shadows. Which is good, because I don't need to see everything all at once. I need to go gently into these abandoned parts of me.

More and more, my group activities involve real people. Which kind of sucks because real people were the problem, or rather, I assumed they were. The problem being I picked the wrong people. I jumped onto the carousel and tried to ride it out with the Four Horsemen. Each time believing it was not me. It was. I was allowing the wrong types of love and showing them it was ok. Showing them that their hurtful words and actions were fine because there was still love. Love looked like: threatening to throw me down the stairs, raging at me, throwing things in my direction, holes in walls, drug overdoses and drinking (that were my fault), stating I did not have to give consent because being engaged was an open invitation at any time, telling me the things that made someone uncomfortable were because I am mentally ill. It was me all along. I am not excusing these actions. That shit sucked. But the common thread was me. By allowing these things for the sake of love, I let it be ok. When I knew it was not. We show people how to love us. I showed people I thought love looked like abuse.

When I am not trying to hold hands with apocalyptic demons, I receive actual love. Love pure, deep, blissful. Love that shows up with hugs, and smiles, and companionship. Love that when I ask for help, it shows up. That part really freaks me out. That people will respond to my cries for help simply because they want to. I spent so long figuring things out on my own that I forgot even how to ask for help. It gives me anxiety to even ask a barista for a glass of water. It feels like an extreme sport: get up, walk 10,000 years across the desert with 1,000 eyes looking and judging me, get to the counter, wait in line, or even worse - not wait in line, look as sorry as I possibly can for bugging them, maybe audibly apologize for bugging them, ask for the free glass of water, walk the journey of 10,000 years all over again. So, you see, asking for help with anything, asking for company is a miracle I make every time I do it. An even bigger miracle is, people respond. Every time, they respond, and I really have maybe never heard no. The lunatics! I have no idea why they want to help me. Why they hang out with me. Why sometimes people even come to my house. My house has me in it, don't they know?! It is also summer, so my trash and sponges smell all the time. How come anyone is willing to walk into a building that has me and my smelly trash sponges? Those *lunatics*!

I really need more lunatics in my life. They help me to help myself stay whole. Sometimes I even take my trash out more often so later I'm not hanging out with trash sponges either. They put cracks in my walls so large I can't repair them. Even better, I don't want to anymore. Thank God for lunatics.

Loving My Brain

YESTERDAY, I READ almost three pages out of *Leaves of Grass*. This may not seem like a big deal. You may be thinking, 'Yeah, yeah, I don't have time to read either'. Time is not the problem. I have plenty of time during my day. I have a brain injury and suspected CTE. Which means my brain cells don't work at the rate they use to. Reading has become something I am unable to do most days. It either makes me want to throw up or is so much on my brain that I can't focus. The words become nothing I recognize. The pages become hard to hold. So almost three pages, where a week ago I could read none, is a fantastic thing for me.

Small tasks have become large mountains these days. The art of getting dressed, maybe putting in laundry or putting away dishes, driving, being out in public, showering, remembering to eat; they are huge tasks now. They drain my energy. Whoever said energy can not be created or destroyed, did not have a brain injury. It also just took me minutes and a Google search to figure out how to spell destroyed. By around 7:30 every night, I am so ready for bed. If I have had an exhausting day, I get even more confused than usual. I forget what I have and have not done. Getting dressed for bed becomes so hard that I sometimes have to give up and try again in a few minutes. Thank goodness no one is around to watch me struggle blindly in my sideways nightgown. The cats don't care, they get lost in clothing too. I have a hard time figuring out if I have done all the steps to complete a shower.

It is frustrating, and I can't pretend that every day I meet this frustration with a lot of grace. Sometimes I yell or cry or curse my new situation. Then I remember that in some ways, I have been given a gift. I now take it day by day. I can not do too much planning until the day of because I won't know until then what my limit is. I have to keep stress at a low level instead of my usual sucking it up. I have to choose wisely about who I spend my time with. The brain is like outer space in our bodies. No one knows for sure how this will progress. Maybe I will be fine. Maybe my brain cells are dying at a faster rate and I will eventually have dementia. Maybe the injury won't take me down but my genetic predisposition of having dementia will. Time will tell. Life is a death sentence handed out to everyone. I am just more aware of how I spend my time and who I spend it with. I may not have time to wait for the people who are not sure if I fit in their life. I worry that I will become too much for anyone to be around. Then I remember, I cannot rob people of making that choice on their own. I have to let them decide how much they can handle.

Since my brain is a little 'off' now, my memory not so great, my balance even worse, I try and pass out often; I may not be able to go back to the job I had. I loved my job, my coworkers, the ladies in the group home I supported. I also know it may be a veiled gift. I get to pick exactly what to do with my time. I may be able to go into business (wow, what a hard word to spell!) for myself and therefore have a schedule that works so much better for where I am each day. I will get to go at my own pace. Have the time to do the slowing down I require.

Some days, I do mourn the loss of the life I had. Most days, I am thrilled that I now have to be more careful. Recognize I have limits that are different than what they were. My brain has given me permission to no longer feel bad about needing to slow down and not try and do everything. My new journey may have thrown me directly onto the path I really was meant to be on. Who knows how many days I have, but then again, no one really ever knows how much time they have. I am thankful I get to be more aware of this than most people. That I have been forced to be more direct, be more deliberate, slow down and breathe when I have to. I get to enjoy little things so much more now. Celebrate things that I was taking for granted. Thank you, universe, for the gift of a better life. I may not love every moment, but every moment, I will have love. I choose love. Every. Moment.

What My Rescue Cats and a Child Taught Me About Consent

At one point in my life, I was volunteering at a cat shelter. Yeah, we all know how this story ends; I took some of the cats home. That part took a while. I never went in to volunteer with the intention of taking one home. Then one day, I went into the shelter with the intention of adopting a cat. It was a day I was not volunteering, and after spending time in each of the rooms, time with some of the animals, I did not connect with any one of them the way I wanted.

One of the people working there brought me up to the FIV+ room and encouraged me to spend some time with a cat named Sally. I had spent a lot of time around her when volunteering. She was a very sweet, shy, tiny cat. She was also older, and I wasn't sure I could fall in love with a cat who only had a few years. So, I walked around the room a little bit. On top of one of the crates was a fluffy tabby cat who was pretty asleep. I had never seen him before and was curious. I put my hand out to pet him and he opened his eyes, started purring, and rubbed his head against me. A few minutes later, I sat down on the floor and he instantly jumped down to sit in my lap. I wanted to see if he would allow me to pick him up. When I did, the fucking cat threw his arms around my neck and put his head on my shoulder. I was done for. He had picked me, and I was ruined for life with my love for this animal.

This cat was found in a garage, herding a litter of kittens. He came to the shelter with skin sores and was very beaten up. He also had a lot of rules about where he could be touched. No sides, no stomach, no feet. I have owned him for years now and some of his rules have let up. His feet are still off limits. Everywhere else I am allowed to pet for a small amount of time. He knows he can trust me. He also sleeps most nights either underneath the blankets with my arms wrapped around him or he smushes his face so close to mine I think he is trying to crawl in.

The next cat that picked me, I think, is full of demons. She has the weirdest personality I have ever seen in a cat. She will get crazy eyes and run around, try to climb walls. When she needs attention, she will yell a little and fall over like she has been shot. She will do this until you pet her. She also plays fetch with hair ties better than the family dog did.

She has taught me the most about consent. Like most animal people, I really like to crush my cats with love. I walk up to them and smash their faces with kisses. With her, she backs away whenever I do this. I understand because her owners before me pierced her ears and she isn't so keen on people getting close to her face. What I have learned is that if I walk up to her, look her right in the eye, and tell her I am going to kiss her head she has no problem. She doesn't back away or look freaked out. She lets me, happily. I in no way think she understands English [13] . I do think that she understands I am not about to hurt her, and I am speaking to her gently, so she isn't surprised by what I am about to do.

With both of these animals, I have been shown time and time again that it is okay to set boundaries, still get needs met, and no one is going to be upset if some backing off needs to be done. They teach me every day that a level of trust needs to be established before anything outside of the comfort zone can be approached.

My cats and myself have had trust broken by humans we thought were going to take care of us. My cats know better than I do that it is ok to take time for trust to be established with anyone new. That their limits are important and may change. I look to nature a lot to teach me the things I have forgotten. I try and overthink, complicate what is simple. Nature has it all figured out and is blessed to not have a human mind to muddle what is true. I hope everyone in the world experiences the love of an animal that has been cast aside by humanity. They know when they are finally safe and home. Even broken rescue animals choose to believe that there is good in humanity and they will be loved.

The other lesson I learned came one Easter. I was hiding in a closet with my cousin's then two-year-old daughter. If you are asking why we were in a closet, you have clearly never been around children. We were looking at the coats, and she screamed when she got to the purple one because she loved it. We made animals noises and pretended no one knew where we were. At one point, this little tiny

---

[13] *I do.*

angel princess looked up at me. She smiled and said, "I like you face. Can I kiss it?" and then…. she waited! A two-year-old knows better than most grown ass adults that if you ask to kiss someone, you need to wait for an answer first. I try as much as I can to ask someone if I can hug them or touch them in anyway first. I think it is considerate. It also took me almost thirty years to bring that practice into my life. Children are sometimes a lot smarter than adults.

Waking Up and Still Having a Brain Injury

WHEN TALKING TO FRIENDS about my brain disease, I am met with some pity, some support, and sometimes words of 'hey, I have some insight on acceptance that I would love to share with you'. The acceptance people are trying to help. They have lessons they want to share in hopes I will be able to get the same things out of what they know. I like that I have people who are so willing to share their knowledge with me. Sharing is a very good practice. I love sharing ideas, activities, dreams, food, really everything except my bed most nights. I also sometimes *really* want to yell at the sharing people.

Like this morning when I woke up and walked into my living room to discover that I left a candle burning all night. I forgot to blow it out. I forgot because I forget things all the time. Mostly I forget stupid little things. Sometimes I forget things I have set on fire and that could be dangerous. This morning, I want to shove the messages of acceptance back down their throats and tell them I could have burned to death because I wasn't careful, and I am by myself. This morning, when my head was screaming in pain as a constant reminder that I do have something not great going on in my brain, I do not want to choose acceptance. I do not want to meet this shitty situation with grace. I am terrified, tired, fed up, and feel like I cannot try and explain all of that to one more person. I do not want to accept these things. I do not want to pretend it is okay that I am okay, and I am happy.

Within moments of waking up, I was reminded I have dangerous limits. That my independence may kill me in a fire from a discounted Yankee Candle. Right now, I don't need messages of joy coming at me like a door to door salesman [14] and Eckhart Tolle levels of acceptance. Right now, I need a witness. I need it to be okay that I am not okay. I need to be able to air out the ugly of how I am feeling and have it be fine that I am not radiating shiny and happy. I cannot spend every day keeping other people comfortable when I am writhing in my head. I am thankful for another day that I have been able to wake up, but my goodness, am I currently not thankful that I am met with so many limits. I do think I could find enough strength to shove acceptance somewhere the sun will never dare to go and then sit back with my tea and a small smile. Today, I think I'm going to not accept that this is it for me. I am not going to accept that I have pseudo-dementia and therefore am a much different, lesser version of myself. I actually refuse to do that today. I did not fight so hard for my life only to have this get the best of me.

---

[14] *Or maybe online salesman these days. Overpriced leggings/essential oils/vitamins anyone?*

Grey Ideas in a Black And White Mind

WE LIVE IN A TIME where everything is at our fingertips. For me, I choose to have my social media slammed with words of inspiration, Disney on magic mushroom levels of 'good vibes'. Some of them show up exactly when I need to hear them. Some of them I have heard over and over again that I believe them as my own truth.

If you are anything like me, I work in extremes. So, when I am told the best way to get out of your own sadness is to help someone else, I help everyone else except for me. Then comes another banner saying the best remedy is to focus on myself. I try. The first message of helping others makes me feel selfish which means I go back to helping everyone else. This is an exhausting cycle that I get stuck in. It causes me to full steam ahead at other people's problems. I then get burned out, try and focus on myself more, feel like I don't need it as badly as other people, go and help someone, remove, repeat, repeat.

The most honest message for me is that one that tells people something along the lines of, 'the person who looks like they don't need help often needs the most support'. How true this has been for me. The more people I reach out my support to, the more I usually need it. The more time I spend looking shiny, happy, and whole, the more I don't feel any of that.

I was given the message that for anyone to be ok, I had to be perfect. If I was only good enough, the drug addictions, depression, suicide, and deadly health issues would all fall away. If I could only be good enough, the rest of the world would be too. I don't remember a time where I didn't believe this. Big shock, I was never really able to be a kid. I have gaps in the things I know how to do. There really wasn't time to learn how to ride a bike, whistle, or cut food properly[15]. I was so busy saving the world.

This caused me to trade emotions for an act of happy. Oh yeah, a long history of abuse really doesn't help either. The message people deliver of letting your feelings pass doesn't work. Letting things pass translates in my head to ignoring the feeling so you don't feel it. At one time, not feeling anything meant I was still safe. That if I was not feeling myself get ripped apart, it would be easier to put myself back together once it was over. I need to learn how to do the opposite. I need to welcome in anger, sadness. I need to *feel* all of this. Actually, feel all of the emotions instead of 'letting them go'. I'm not afraid that I will never be able to stop feeling one of them once I let myself. I am more afraid of continuing to never feel any of them. To never live so fully that I don't really know any emotions. Because then, I also will never learn happy, love, joy.

---

[15] *Not saving the world anymore. Still can't do any of these things. I've definitely never seen Batman ride a bike either soo....*

For anyone that has given away so much of themselves because they were told it would help you be whole, I see you. I understand. I do not want to send out a message of 'it will get better' or 'we can do hard things'. How about instead I use my battle cry to say fuck all this god-awful shit that is in the world. That some days I do not trust God, the Universe, Science, The Great Big Beyond Whatever to be in charge of those I love. I also know I can't do it on my own.

Dementia Land

AS I UNPACK my things, I am instantly struck with how much I do not belong in this room. The room I was never allowed in as a child. It seems to be telling me I still don't belong here. All of my belongings seem too colorful, too modern, too much. There are too many patterns, too much plastic, and nothing of me could ever hope to look right among the dust, and wood, and books. Books so old, the words are barely contained in their covers any more. Even my clothing, as earth toned as they are, seem to stick out and yell that there is an intruder. Someone has come and disrupted the dust and memories that have been kept safe, untouched for so long.

Photographs of the deceased family watch as I struggle to find a place for my 2014 life in a 1950's world. The rest of the house is a museum. The stories that line the walls could fill a history museum. Tales of my family coming to this life. I am surrounded by souvenirs from wars fought, trips around the world, my ancestors coming to this town, the story of how even I ended up here. Pocket watches that still wind and tick, opera glasses that witnessed notes float about the rafters, rosaries that kept secret prayers, my grandmother's music box that still plays on. Relics from my own history. They all help to guard the house. I am Rod Serling about to embark on a long-forgotten corner of the Twilight Zone.

Friends and family have stopped showing up and have been replaced by nice strangers with faces that look exactly like relatives. There is somehow always money, food, heat and the lights stay on, though bills do not pass hands in this house. The actors in the TV are always too loud or too soft, and how frustrating must it be for them to say the same advertisements over and over again. They never leave and there are no cameras.

Today, I am not stronger than my grandmother's dementia. As she is thumbing through her rolodex trying to make the names and numbers make sense. She is hoping for the company of her family. I am not bigger than this. I hand her a glass of wine that has been so watered down it may just be juice at this point. It helps with the sadness of missing her family. What she will never know again is that her family is always with her. Making her dinner, cleaning up her midnight snack tornados, having conversations with her. She tells me of the passing of her son and how much I would have liked him. She's right, I loved my uncle. She will never know who I am again. I am simply the nice stranger who allows her to live in 'my house'. I am the product of centuries of strong women. It will take all their strength to live in this twisted world where my 88-year-old grandmother has become my 8-year-old child.

Some days, she doesn't even remember she had any children at all. In this new world, I don't exist. When my mother comes to see the person who raised her, they are strangers to each other. When my dad comes, she knows him and loves him. Her mind made up this fantastic story where my dad spent some time inside of her dishwasher. She loves telling this story.

She spent a good portion of her life acting in plays. You can tell because she is so good at convincing doctors that she knows more than she does. Pretending she knows exactly who the people in town are. I think this is the hardest and longest role she's ever played. The pretending that she doesn't live in a Wonderland where lights are terrifying, mysterious men hang out in the carport at night, and water is so frightening that showering/teeth brushing is out of the question. The knobs have been taken off the stove, the microwave works when a secret code is entered that only I have. Lies that have to be reality in order to keep her safe. Ice cream and chips are her two major food groups now. With age comes the loss of taste and smell. Texture and temperature are as close to tasting as she gets.

The small light in a dimming world is the theatre, however. I, too, act in plays. In a small town, we have shared a stage with the same people. People I watched create the magic that drew me onto my first stage. We can talk for hours about this one thing that connects us. About the people we know, how exhilarating it is to hear the audience react to you. I see her eyes light up in a forgotten way talking about being in plays. The last play she ever saw was one I was in. She didn't know I was in it. She asks me if I saw it and wasn't it wonderful. Months later, she still brings up the play. Somewhere in her head, something connects enough to ask me about our fellow thespians. I find DVDs of old musicals for us to watch together. She doesn't like Judy Garland but thinks Liza Minnelli seems very humble. I remember days being home sick from school, she would come over with her copy of The Sound of Music and bribe me with tea and ice cream until I felt better. Funny that I do the same thing with her now and don't even think about it. I didn't know how much I would need theatre until I entered Dementia Land.

I live in her house now without her; well, without her physical body. I know she is here, and she doesn't let me forget for too long. There is new paint, carpets ripped up, the bathroom replaced. This is still her house. The house my grandfather built for their family. Did they know it would be passed down across the generations? I know she is still around when I walk into the house and it all of a sudden smells exactly the way it did when I was younger. That smell is the reason why I like pumpkin spice coffee. It tastes exactly how the house use to smell. Some days, I am hit so hard with that smell that I find it hard to believe she isn't here. That I am not a teenager entering her house for Christmas. No amount of sage or time has been able to get rid of this happening from time to time. I'm not sure I want it to either. She was never that warm grandmotherly type. She didn't shower her grandchildren with affection and cookies. Still, I am certain she is showing up to remind me she loves and supports me in whatever way she knows how. I think she comes around because she knows I gave up my city life in Chicago to live on a dirt road in Dementia Land with her. I think she is trying to say thank you.

Dear Body,

I FUCKING HATE YOU. You have given up on me time and time again. I wish I could just shape you like clay into the form I would like you to be. I hate you for all the stares you get from people, for allowing yourself to be taken over by other human bodies, for the fact that you may never be able to have kids, which is a basic function of being female.

I try and be outside of you as much as I can. I hate any connection I have with you. You are sick and disgusting. I wish I could shed you as easily as my clothing. I am not sorry for all the abuse you have put up with because of me. I feel like you deserve it., you're not worth much more.

I've tried to accept you, cut you out of my life, rip you apart, burn you up, shrink you, decorate you. Still, I hate you. I'm still trapped inside the thing I hate most in this world.

Dear Katie,

I'M SORRY I'VE let you down. You have been no picnic for me, either. You have ripped me open, bled me out, shrank me, starved me, over-exercised me, and have tried to remove my life. I'm doing the best I can. It just hasn't been enough for you. Now I have the scars to show for it. Maybe one day we can find a way to coexist.

Dear Bowling Ball of Sadness,

I carry you around with me everywhere. You cause me to not want to eat and make me feel like I am constantly expanding. At this point, you are almost a quarter of a century old and I think it is time for me to drop you. I think I will be lonely without you for a little while. I will also be better without you. It Is really hard for me to feel you fully. I think I have to in order to move on and feel better; feel anything. You have served your purpose and I appreciate that. I can't play victim to my trauma anymore. I want to be able to move on and live my life; happy, joyous, and free. I want to be able to take back my own sadness, hurt, pain, and anger. I want to finally feel them instead of having them all expand in my stomach or take the emotions out on myself. You have turned me into a monster and it needs to stop immediately. Now. I need to be safe in my own body and right now, I am not. Once I am rid of you, I will be able to stop destroying myself. I don't deserve to feel like this. I never have. You are weighing me down with the only weight I will ever need to lose. You are not keeping me safe or protected. You serve me in absolutely no way. I am taking

back my life and my body. My ability to feel emotions is
coming with me. I will not allow you to sink me.

Dear Everyone Who was Too Afraid to Love Me,

THANK YOU. Because of you, I finally had to love myself.

Energy Healing

THESE DAYS, WE compliment people on their energy. Like humans have a choice to be either oil or solar powered people. Sun people or dark abysses. We are obsessed with the energy things give off. People can send 'good vibes only' and shun anyone driving a Prius. Maybe they are just mad they have to get gas more than once a month. Or the gas station attendant is one of the only people they see regularly so they like taking the trip. You can be a giant asshole, and if you live off the grid, you are made a savior.

I think there is an entire generation of people who missed the science lesson telling us that energy cannot be created or destroyed. This whole energy thing has been here the whole time. Long before the world even really came to be. We shoved wires into the ground to harness it. It use to be used to light the way. Not to light our cell phones, so we don't have to talk to anyone. We can hide behind inspirational messages so that our energy looks great. Even when we can't get out of bed. Our internet personality tells the world of the great energy we are letting into the universe. We take pictures of vegan / organic / sustainable /

whatever buzz word we like right now. Pretend that the farmer is not as important as the cow he keeps. That doesn't seem like 'good vibes' to me.

We decided to storm onto video channels telling the tale of how chakras and energy healing are the new lifesaving thing. Like the new Columbus, discovering something that has existed far longer than we ever will. We didn't create energy, we won't leave any behind. What we leave is going to be a mess. Hopefully some good in the process. I think the secret to life is that we are not necessary (at all) for it to keep going.

Competition VS Perfectionism

I DON'T BELIEVE that competition and perfectionism are even close to the same thing. They look very similar. Certainly, perfectionism can cause competition. In competition, there is an end goal, a desire to be better than the top person, or at least better than we were. Competition can be friendly games or angry determination to beat out someone else.

Perfectionism, to me, looks nothing like this. It says that before I even begin, I have to know every single outcome. I need every detail of all the information I can find. I have to be ready and be an expert before even starting. A lot of times, this means I don't even start. If I can't know everything beforehand, anxiety rears up and I resist. What if I am not good at this new thing as soon as I start it? Worse, what if I am good at it but I'm not the best? Perfectionism tells me I can't even go swimming. I don't look good enough in a swimsuit. Being in water feels like I can't breathe. If I can't see the bottom, really see what I am jumping in to, I flat out refuse to go in the water. Which is funny considering I love being near water. On the edges of it. Never in it.

I've lived my life a lot like I am swimming. Never fully jumping in. Not taking chances because I can't see the whole thing first. I stay at the edges of people, activities, feelings. Since I can't know all the pieces of the puzzle first. I don't want to begin sorting it out. I am too afraid that I will not be enough, or be too much, or not right, or look silly.

If life really is a puzzle, my biggest fear is that I am working on the wrong one. I will complete the entire life's work. The final piece will be me. I will not fit together with all the other perfectly-shaped and colored pieces. I am always afraid that I will be wrong. That I AM wrong.

Sometimes I get glimpses of myself without perfectionism. I am reckless and go in full force with a heart of faith. Yes, I have sometimes gotten hurt, bumped around. My goodness though, what a crazy beautiful ride it is to jump in with both feet and just see what happens.

Oh yes, I also came to this idea while I was sitting in a meditation group, imperfectly meditating on the idea of being perfect at mediating. What a mind I have.

The Making of a Monster

I RAN INTO a friend the other day on the train, and there it was again. Right in the middle of our "philosophizing" about our family units around the holiday season, he told me that no matter what, he knows that I will always be ok. This phrase, or some variation (i.e. 'you are the most put together person I know') has followed me for as long as I can remember. I used to thank people or giggle or roll my eyes, but in later years, I have taken to politely smiling and excusing myself to the bathroom where I can throw up and question my existence, or at least other people's existence, on the bathroom floor. I guess 'put together' looks different to everyone else than I thought it would be. Funny thing though, I have tried to be a 'real and normal person' and I am so not put together when I do that. Somehow, the not eating/peering into the magic mirror that is the toilet bowl, keeps me more whole. At my best (worst if you want to look at it that way) times I was doing a really nice job taking care of myself. I'd make sure every hair was in place, my make-up perfection, skin always moisturized, nails done, clothes up to date. In the times I would let myself go (recovery), I would not shower for days, wouldn't brush my hair, sometimes would even wear all my underwear inside out to avoid laundry; I don't do grey areas very well. It should go without saying that the use of my gym membership suffered similar abuse or neglect.

I guess so far, I have sounded as if I really enjoyed my eating disorder. I did. It made me feel superhuman. The combination of having no food in your stomach and whatever caffeine (diet) pill I was abusing at the time made my entire body vibrate. I had this constant energy that kept me upbeat and alert all day every day and usually until 4 am. I would spend my nights replacing sleep with exercise and sometimes pulling everything out of my closet, so I could begin to get rid of more weight. Plus, it felt good to know that I could do all these things and still sit with other people and refuse the same foods they just couldn't help but eat. This is not to say I would recommend this lifestyle to anyone. In fact, I wouldn't wish that on my worst enemy, and I have a few. But for me, when I needed something to hang onto, I reached out and found ED.

Growing up, as a product of my genetics, I was heavy. However, I did not know this. I had no concept of body image or that people might think another human being was fat, or think I was fat for that matter. I remember becoming aware of these facts right around the time most other people realize their lives will never be the same. I was twelve. Up until that point, my friends and I usually spent our time playing with our American Girl dolls and making cookies. This usually resulted in eating a lot of the batter, of course. Then one day, something changed. My best friend and I were standing at my parents' kitchen counter, whipping up our latest batch of extra chocolate chip cookies when… she refused to lick the bowl with me. She said that since we were going to a pool party later that week, she didn't want to be fat in her bathing suit. I really wasn't sure what she meant. How could flour, butter, and chocolate make you fat? Was fat something that could happen overnight? Like while you were sleeping, all of a sudden, the Stay Puff guy crams himself down your throat and you wake up having taken on his shape like a snake would? Wasn't fat only one of those problems adults had to worry about after they had pushed out a few kids and were applying wrinkle cream? I wasn't convinced, so I licked the bowl.

I do recall my mother at various points trying to say something to the effect of how she had been the chubby one growing up and she would discourage me from snacking in between school and dinner. I still do not know if she was trying to relate with me or keep me from expanding outward. I'm still not sure… the best laid plans or something like that.

It wouldn't be until months later that I would really have any cause to consider the fat question again. I came down with the flu just as signs of the first and only growth spurt I would ever have showed up. The combination caused me to come out the other side much skinnier than I had been previously, something my mother was quick to notice as well as the cesspool of hormones that is every young teenage boy. I would date my first two boyfriends that year. Unfortunately, they were also best friends and their 'love' for me put a rift in their friendship, not before they began to place bets with each other on which one of them I would date. Feeling like a racehorse was strike one for me. While battling my own hormones, I discovered a brand-new feeling known as depression. My parents would try and get me to talk to a therapist, but I was uncooperative, so they kept having to find new ones. I had friends, after all, so what was a stranger going to do for me that they couldn't?[16]

The thing about growing into your body and having no concept of body image is that you constantly walk around with a very high level of confidence, which tends to make you look older. I was beginning to notice that everywhere I went, there were always people, usually older men, outright staring at me. This would be strike two for me as I would constantly be checking myself in mirrors or windows to make sure I didn't have something on my face or toilet paper on my shoe or perhaps my skirt tucked into my underwear (really all things I had only seen in movies, but you never know). I, however, could never find anything wrong so I was starting to wonder what exactly it was about my appearance that was wrong. This phenomenon still happens to me everywhere I go. I did spend some time thinking I had made it all up in my head and was just being self-centered that I thought people were looking but it would be confirmed to me one day at college when I was walking across campus with an acquaintance, who commented how much he liked walking around with me because of all the stares.

---

[16] *Please go to therapy. It really helps.*

The third and final strike would come in the form of a vice principal at my middle school. He was new that year and very... involved. I spent a very glorious night in an emergency room one day because my English teacher at the time mistook a fictional writing assignment for a suicide note. I was dragged out of school and forced to answer questions that I didn't think I should be asked in the first place. One nicer psychology student told me that if I didn't start to corporate, they would admit me, and the other people in the psych ward were actually crazy. I cooperated. Because of this, the vice principal decided to check up on me. Around the same time one of the girls in my circle of friends was going through a rough patch of an abusive father and her parents splitting up. He would call us down to his office to chat. Now, when I was in middle school, the cool thing to do was to decorate a notebook and pass it around to your closest friends to write to each other in. Caveman text messaging for you, young folk. Our notebook led to the discovery that the vice principal was getting far too close to both of us. My friend was too shy to ever say anything about how uncomfortable it was that he told us to come see him any time and wrote a song for the talent show that sounded too similar to things he had said to us. The breaking point was when he called my parents. He was updating them on my 'progress' and told my mom I was a lovely girl with a very nice body. Well slap a wig on me and call me Bertha if that wasn't inappropriate! My mom was very good friends with someone on the Board of Education, so she passed this onto her. The slag only got a slap on the wrists and a promotion as principal of the elementary school. Years later, I would be babysitting and hear one of the girls say to their mother how the principal was bringing her into his office and she didn't like it. Her mother brushed it off as a student not liking their authority, but a red flag went up inside me and I mentioned to their mom that she should be wary. As far as I know, he still is principal at that school.

At this point, I was done with trying to cope well. Only I didn't know it. They say that people with eating disorders are in denial. What they mean is they are in denial with themselves. It took me many, many years to realize what I was doing. I thought I was just never hungry, so I never ate. My friends and I used to eat in our teachers' classrooms instead of the cafeteria and our favorite one would refuse to let me eat with her unless I actually ate. My French teacher took it to a whole new level one day. I really have no idea how bad I looked or if I had not been eating. I thought I was fine, but she disagreed because she dragged me out of my desk and into the lunch line to buy food, holding my wrist the entire time to make sure I did it. I thought they were being silly and overprotective. I wasn't hungry, I didn't eat. In my defense, I did spend my entire grade school years having a lunch period somewhere between 10-11am every day, so who could blame me? That is a stupid time for lunch.[17]

They say that eating disorders are a coping mechanism. That the people who find ED do not actually

---

[17] *There is no stupid time for lunch. Eat lunch. It's delicious. Even the name sounds delicious.*

want to be skinny, they just don't know how to deal with things any other way. In some ways, I know that is true, but I also know that my very first reason for needing ED was because I wanted to disappear. I wanted to be so skinny that I no longer existed. I am not saying that I wanted to die. I wasn't using ED to kill myself. I just didn't want to be seen any more. I didn't want any more eyes looking at me, including my own.

In recovery, they tell you to personify your eating disorder. This is why it is often referred to as ED. A person's name. A lot of people create an image of what ED looks like. Usually ED is a monster. To me, ED is a shapeshifter, never a monster though. ED a lot of times looks like the man of my dreams, if I could build the perfect person to wrap my arms around forever, it would look like ED. Other times, ED is the most perfect woman I have ever seen, the one I want to be so badly that I would die to be her. The most dangerous form ED took was sounding like my friends and family. ED did such an accurate impression of the people I loved, I was convinced that the words in my head were actual words that had come out of their mouths. This was good for ED. It meant that anything those people said in real life, I no longer believed because I knew how they really felt. ED is sometimes the most abusive relationship anyone will ever have. ED convinced me that I could trust no one but ED, that no one loved me or would stay with me except for ED. I believed it, I believed it almost to my grave.

Dear Body
Forgive me.

Dear Body

Forgive me

Dear Body

Forgive me

Dear Body

Forgive me

Dear Body

Forgive me

Dear Body

Forgive me

Dear Body

Forgive me

Dear Body

Forgive me

Dear Body

Forgive me

Dear Body

Forgive me

Part 2

Bodies of Poetry

Make Up Tutorial for a Brain Injury

When I tell the nurse,[18]
'Hey, I tip over if I stand for too long,'
She tells me that sounds bad,
But I have beautiful hair so that should make up for it.
When I tell my friend,
I want to go to sleep at 8 pm,
They tell me I'm being really cute.
Cute looks sad, lonely, tired, and fed up.
When I stand in the grocery store aisle,
Staring at the Fig Newtons,
Trying to remember if I like them,
A stranger walks by and tells me,
'I'm too pretty not to smile'.
I put on make-up every day,
So, I don't look like that's the only thing I was able to do all
    day.
With some eyeshadow and highlighter,
I cover up every night I have spent crying in the shower,
Because I can't remember if I have washed my hair.
When I look pretty,
It is so no one can see I'm scared,
Scared that the man I love will not be brave enough,
That he will still love me,
Even when I forget my keys, my clothes,

---

[18] *Nurses are really great. Don't discount them. I was raised by nurses.*
They are heroes. Go find a nurse and hug them.

And his name.
 I wonder,
Who will bear witness,
To my hands forgetting how to use a fork,
And my mind no longer understanding,
It's okay,
At least you are beautiful.

Paint the Town Red

Can you imagine what happened
The day the first fire was discovered?
How fingertips drew flames
Magic at the beginning of the world.
Centuries of shaman looking closely
To glean from the blue, and red, and orange tongues
The words of things to come.
A cow in Chicago
Kicking over one single flame
And tipping a city into its second coming.
In California
Where ancient trees and new families are snuffed out as
    one
South Dakota sweat lodges
New England hearths
Witches and bread used as one.
Teenagers sneaking out of windows
To learn what the fire knows
Pictures, love letters, herbs
Burned and buried as ghosts.
A match is lit
A life starts double
Sparks of creation
Original magic
The eternal flame.

Secrets Keep Us Sick

Locked in your cage of the most mortal limitations,
You set bets,
And aim to win,
Each time moving further into the fog.
Where secrets scream,
Not whisper.
But don't let them out,
Don't show the cards you hold,
The joker isn't laughing in here.

Colder, darker, deeper,
You are dragged down,
Further down,
Each win brings you closer,
And further.

The secrets scream,
Not whisper.

The bones shake in the cold,
Solidifying the bet,
Everything is blue circles and pale lines,
The beautiful vibrating of your own noise,
You will win this game yet.

You are so far down now,
No one can touch you,
Push again,
Play the final card.

Your secrets scream,
They will never whisper.

Seam. Less.

One day,
And I don't know when,
Your name will not be the first name my lips remember,
Your heart will not be the heart I have made room for.
One day,
And I don't know when,
The spaces I opened in order to fit you,
Will shift and shape into another.
And this time,
The space will be mine.
Today is not that day,
I clean my house,
As if the memory of you,
Is hiding in the motes of dust,
Brought on by a summer we'll never share.
I replace the sounds of your sleeping,
With the sounds of my computer.
Because today is not that day,
I still expect you to take up room in the space I made for
    you.
Because today is not that day,
I still forget sleep,
Over worry about where you are,
Your mind and your body,
Traveling on two different planes,
So far apart,
I could never find thread long enough to touch both.

Because today is not that day,

My arms reach out and around to find you.

Like I ever had you.

One day,

And I don't know when,

It won't be your voice that soothed and scared me,

Ripping me to pieces thinner than your guitar strings that I
    danced on.

One day,

And I get to pick when,

The only voice I will hear,

Will be my own.

Preface to the Stories I'm Not Supposed to Tell

They sat us down with plates piled high
In view of locked kitchens and bathrooms
Telling us to use each other as mirrors
And write affirmations on the real ones.

The first time I saw bravery
It was tears from someone eating sugar for the first time in
    four years
It was her birthday.
The first cry of freedom
Came from a girl who electrocuted herself
So, she wouldn't enter her kitchen.

With Tom Hanks
We discovered that there were enough rocks
If we could only use them as weapons
Instead of weight.

I have howled at the moon
Finger painted in my emotions
Danced like Kevin Bacon when we weren't supposed to.
I was given the gift of everything
From women who thought they had nothing left inside of
    them.

We stopped kissing monsters
No longer chased after skeletons
Discovered that with lighters and paper
Fire could cleanse our souls.

My life sisters,
I hope your skin still charges in the moonlight
I hope you still breathe dreams
Long may you stomp out sadness in your best boots
And bang your drums wildly, madly, in love.

Living in Recovery

Ellie slowly opened her eyes to the sound of static. As she tried to regain her focus, she realized she was in a pitch-black room with something very tight around her torso and arms. The material was coarse, and as her eyes adjusted to her surroundings, she saw it was white. When she moved, buckles tinkled lightly. A straight jacket. The harder she thrashed, the more constricting the jacket became. Ellie screamed until all of her energy gave out. She wasn't sure if the temperature of the room changed or her body itself did. All of a sudden, Ellie was sweating. She struggled for many hours. Her body eventually went limp, giving in to her exhaustion.

She stayed for many hours in the dark, alternating between struggling and giving up. When it seemed she would be trapped forever, she discovered something. A small hole just big enough for her pinky in one of the jacket sleeves. She wiggled her finger through and started to pull. It was a slow process. Finally, Ellie ripped through.

Just as the last shreds of material dropped to the floor, the world gave out, or so it seemed. There was a rush of wind and a loud roar. Suddenly there was no floor, and Ellie dropped into a dark pool of water. Deeper and deeper she fell. It felt like an eternity. She struggled to figure out which way was up. More importantly, she tried with all of her might to not swallow any of the water.

The longer she stayed under, the more hopeless things became. Finally, things started to go foggy except for a light that appeared. Ellie weakly swam toward the light and realized she was approaching a door. She pushed, water and light poured out around her. The darkness gave way to a light more blinding than the dark.

Ellie stumbled onto a street of busy cars. She ignored them, trying to catch her breath. Once her energy started to come back, she stood there dripping, and waved down the first car that would take her far away from the nightmare. After an hour, a truck stopped to pick her up. Ellie climbed in and quickly fell asleep.

Ellie slowly opened her eyes to the sound of static. This time, it might not be a dream.

To The Woman You Date Next

A love letter:
When he kisses you for the first time,
I hope he doesn't steal your voice from your mouth,
When he sits with his guitar and sings,
I hope those notes aren't the closest you will ever get to
    learning him.
The first time he says he loves you,
Please love yourself enough to know that's not what he
    means,
His 'I love you' speaks about how he can't love himself,
How you will be the conduit for every emotion he has,
You will hold everything for him,
And when you struggle to keep everything in place,
Yours and his,
You will no longer be enough.
I hope I'm wrong,
I hope he's better when he finds you,
I hope my prayers are enough.
If they aren't,
There is a support group down the road,
For all the women who tried to love someone,
Who know nothing of themselves.

Helen of Toyland

When I walk in the room,
You can hear the necks snap,
To gaze at the face,
That revs 100-speed boat engines.
Piles of Sperry shoes and polo shirts drown me.
They ache to peer into the looking glass of my mind,
Back off once they discover what is there,
I am not the girl they will take home,
I am the one their mothers warned about.
They are thrown off balance,
To learn I stand on my own feet,
Blood boils in their veins,
To learn I will not do as I am told.
They retreat from my challenge,
Cover buttons so I can't push them.
I am not the arm decoration they hoped for,
Won't mold to their clay,
Refuse to be sifted down to nothing.
I will not be the calm in their sails,
I will not go quietly into their night.
When they know me,
They will understand,
Why storms are always named,
After people.

Reach For the Stars

When I was younger I was taken outside,
I asked the stars forgiveness,
For help.
When I was older,
I discovered the constellations on your skin,
And hoped the stars would save you too.
When I met you,
You were so lost in space,
You could only see the night,
When I met you,
You mistook scars for falling,
And you couldn't stay.
I ask the stars now to navigate you,
To help you find the laughter I first found in you,
I hear you smile in the night sky,
See it in the moon.
I pray it's pull will be like the tide,
I pray you will be pulled into shore.
I was not a compass you could read,
And I fear you won't find one.
The night sets on fire with your screaming,
I am afraid the stars will become black holes.
I found constellations on your skin,
You found danger and darkness on mine.
So deep and so long you have been sucked under,
A shooting star no one could wish on.
I found constellations on your skin,

Maybe next time I will shoot for the trees.

Love Looks

I wasn't sure what love was supposed to look like
So it looked like harsh words
I traded in me for a ring on my finger
That would later be stolen by someone who also didn't
    know love.
Love evolved
Turned into sleepless nights
Panic attacks
Hoping I didn't breathe wrong and cause more anger
Sometimes it was left in a heroin cage on my couch
Or in the hands of someone who would rather hold a gun.
There are woods and games that speak of the monsters I
    tried to kiss
And the monsters did whatever they liked to the body I left
Love blinded my eyes to signs that I wasn't the only one
    coming to the same bed
Tied me to a red chair I insisted was blue.
Love called me to be the statue in their games
An impressive, silent accessory that avoided stairs
Just in case I ended up at the bottom
Told me that the blame was because of my mind
I needed to focus on them more and also stay away.
It started to look like isolated romance
To a public stranger
A sapling bending to demands I could never carry out
I understood why housewives lived off martinis and

Valium

Appearances matter more anyway.

I think once

Maybe

Someone tried to love me with mix-tapes and safety

It's hard to tell

When you mistake a hand for a heart.

The Club

Your invitation will read
'Fuck you even though that has no meaning anymore'
Anguished words will open The Doors to a room full of
    tortured genius.
Folk songs written about a soup can heart
Walls painted in black eye liner
The air vents will surprise you
The whiskey will leave you in such a haze
You'll only see purple as the company gets a holding on
    you.
The oven is very quiet
Should you need a place to rest
Otherwise give your ear to the rebel's cause
Or sit on the dock and launch a few ships.
You will never be younger than this
So in love, you could die for it.

The Episode Where I Re-Work Some Walt Whitman

I delight in myself, and praise the joyful noise of myself,
What I know you shall also know,
Every part of me also is a part of you.
I wander and invite my soul to wander,
I remain still and at ease, observing the miracles in a single
    blade of grass,
The shape of me made from the very same soil and air,
Born out of all the same things,
Hoping to never falter until my last breath.
All I have learned is put away,
Not forgotten,
But frozen on the fingertips of Winter,
I seek out all the good,
Raise voice to all that is bad,
Find what the hawk and ant have always known,
From the spark of creation.
Echoing rooms full of perfumes,
My senses take in what I know,
The dust could lull me into comfort,
But it won't.
This air is not what I am searching,
Though I am in love with the safety,
Instead I fall into the woods,
Vulnerable and naked,
Driven by an ancient madness to be held up by the earth.

My breath creates the early morning meadow mist,
The inhale and exhale, the raging of my blood,
Awakens the bees to establish the world,
Loosened words call up the wind that carried life rain and
    dead leaves,
Light sun kisses and love-root arms,
Solitary trees or group witness to the provoked traffic,
Energizing decomposition,
I rise from the dirt to greet the sun.
Have you thought of the land?
Have you thought out the world?
Have you tried long enough to understand these words?
Gained pride in knowing a song?
Stop these 24-hours long enough to understand the origin
    of songs,
You will own the good of the land and all the stars still left
    to come,
You will no longer accept the second or third of things,
Or look at the world with dead eyes filtered through
    strangers' words,
You will not take anything from me or from anyone,
You will listen from every side and filter on your own.

They Came For Us Before We Knew Ourselves

Somewhere in the past,
There were people afraid of robots taking over,
Did they know?
Can we see it?
They handed each of us personal remotes,
Promising the world at a touch,
Now we stare into palms that look like screens,
Reading answers we don't believe,
Knowing we don't have to know anything.
So, we cry out how we won't be a part of the masses,
The stream won't drag us with it,
We sound just like everyone else,
With enough inspirational quotes, mood music, and good
     lighting,
We shall overcome!
We shall overcome nothing,
Riots give us anxiety,
Anyone willing to speak with words not fed to us,
Is thrown out,
We sit with the reality shows,
Instead of being shown reality.
Each time someone says, 'I am uncomfortable',
They are given a hug and a planet-based cookie,
Because it is a sin to take something from an animal,
Because the farmer is less than this cow.
The robots have won already,

We have plugged ourselves in,

Tuned in so far,

We have tuned out,

We are the accident no one can look away from,

Extract our skin,

And the reports will show,

Oil has replaced blood,

Oceans of caffeine, booze, expensive juice that promises to
    make us bitter.....

Better,

Survival methods are cute hobbies.

Maybe if we stay away from the light long enough,

We will be spit out of Ray Bradbury's nightmares,

Maybe the hunger games will no longer be about

starvation of truth,

Maybe we can join our bionic hands,

To find,

We are human after all.

Part 3:

Girl Goddesses

This letter was written to me by my brother while I was in residential treatment for my eating disorder. He was unable to attend a family weekend, so my mom handed this to me when she arrived:

Kate,

I'm sorry I couldn't make it down there this weekend. I would have liked to have come. There's no way I could've gotten that time off from work. I'm not really rolling in money and that family weekend thing is expensive.

I hope this last month at The Ranch was helpful. I would have loved for you to come home earlier, but I'm glad Mom and Dad could make this last month happen. I'm happy that you'll be home in a couple of weeks because you being gone for this long has been totally shitty.

I know you hear all the time about how people like you and I hurt the ones we love the most, and most of the time don't even realize it. You didn't need to be told that because you had the pleasure of having a fucking up, alcoholic brother, but it's a true statement. Let me tell you how true that is.

I would say for the past several months, every time I'm at work and my phone vibrates in my pocket, I think of you. I think how I hope it's not Mom calling to tell me that you're hurting yourself in some way, that you've tried to kill yourself, or that you've succeeded this time. And if Dad's name shows up on the caller ID, I can legitimately feel my heart race in my chest because Dad only calls when something serious is going on and my mind consistently jumps to the worst-case scenario every fucking time.

I know that you had most of these feelings when I was going through some of my worst times so this might not be news to you, but sometimes it's better to hear this shit from someone besides a counselor or parent.

I'm scared that you'll somehow get stuck in that vicious cycle of living most of your life in and out of institutions. They're great for the help that they offer, but I think once someone gets too used to being in a facility and that becomes normal, that person has a big problem. I couldn't even tell you how many times I've seen that happen.

It's a gift from God that we both got the parents that we did. Every time I speak at a meeting, I tell everyone that if I had to pick two parents from the entire population of the world, I'd pick ours every single fucking time. The amount of help that we both got from them is staggering, whether we knew it at the time or not.

But, here's the real dope. Open up your Big Book to page 97 and read the last paragraph into the middle of page 98.

That last paragraph has been burned into my consciousness since I read it for the first time. I don't know if you've gotten through steps two and three. If not, now is probably a good time. I don't know if the word 'god' is something that you're comfortable with yet, but it would be a really good time to get right with that as well.

I don't even want to throw this at you because you're my little sister and not some alcoholic dope fiend motherfucker from a meeting, but it's time. I heard years ago that God will meet us halfway. God never transported me to a meeting, took the whiskey out of my hand, or slapped the keys out of the ignition before I drove a car blacked out. He never broke my phone before I called the dealer or forced my anti-depressants down my throat when I refused to take them.

What did happen was I was able to realize that, in general, my will and desires are shit. Totally destructive tendencies that get me in trouble most of the time I act on them. I had to keep it really simple in the beginning and realize that often, God's will for me is the exact opposite of my own. God wouldn't want me to hurt myself or anyone else which means I can't live the way I was living before because whether I knew it or not, I was killing myself and systematically tearing Mom and Dad's hearts out of their chests.

Pray. Pray for the will to live because even if your will isn't to live, whatever you're praying to wants that for you. If you don't want to live for yourself, fake it for a while and live for Mom and Dad until you've found some worth for yourself. Pray more. And then more. If you haven't found something to believe in yet, borrow mine for a day.

The stuff you're battling kills people every day. If this kills you, whether it be suicide, or a slower and more agonizing way, there will be so many lives that will never be the same. Think about how everyone felt when Karen killed herself. Even the cousins would be a wreck.

I'll be honest, there have been more days that I care to admit that I stayed alive for someone else. Mom, Dad, you, whatever poor girl I was dating at the time. Do whatever the fuck it takes.

The flip side of that is that if you get better, there's lots of cool shit out there to do. You can get a job, some healthy friends that care about you, read more books, be in more plays and get more tattoos. You can get more cats and stupid little rodents, string together a few days that don't involve agonizing emotional pain.

Honestly, and I say this a lot, if I felt as bad now as I did nine or ten years ago, I'd be dead. No questions asked. But, I don't. I have good days, and some days that are so good that they make me wonder how I ever thought I couldn't get better.

I fucking love you and so do lots of other people. Ask for help, take the help, and then help yourself. God helps those who help themselves. Now, stop crying and give Mom a hug because I'm sure she's sitting right there. I love you.

She Goes On

MY JOURNEY to The Ranch in Nunnelly, Tennessee, did not begin by seeking out The Ranch. After months of searching, I entered to a program at Silver Hill in Connecticut, a part of the state that might as well be in New York. I don't remember the intake, I don't even remember any of the groups we participated in. What I remember are the people.

I started out in the medical unit of Silver Hill. Everyone starts here to make sure they are medically stable enough and sober enough to begin saving their own life. We were allowed outside for fifteen minutes four times a day. Outside meant we hung out on a cement patio that was surrounded with shatter-proof glass, mesh wire, and bushes so big you couldn't see over them.

In this cement prison, we smoked, listened to music, and practiced a weird version of yoga invented to keep us moving and laughing. It was really nothing like being outside, and if it was raining, we didn't go at all. I think it was one of the few times any of us felt normal.

While I was there, I became very close with two people, David and Annie. We spent as much time as we could together, trying to make the best out of the situation. One day, I was talking about how my depersonalization caused me to understand my body was in one place, however, it usually felt like I was sitting somewhere else entirely, watching everything happen. Instead of being concerned or asking too many questions like most people, Annie got very excited and told me it sounded like I had a superpower. This was the first time anyone had found some good in my DID symptoms.

I spent two weeks in Silver Hill's medical unit before they told me that they were not planning on moving me into one of their programs. It has been decided that, since my PTSD/DID caused disassociation and depersonalization, they did not feel like I would be safe on their campus. I was furious. Why had I just spent so much time here if I was just going to be moved? I was told they had secured me a spot at The Ranch, so I would be getting on a plane to Tennessee. I was not happy. Tennessee was far and meant I would have to start all over again. I also had never heard of this place, so I felt unprepared.

My mom came with me for the plane ride. I can only imagine how hard it was for her. As soon as we got to the airport in Tennessee, I was met by a heavily bearded man holding a sign with my name on it. My mom had to hand me off to this stranger and hope I would be ok. She turned right around and got back on another plane headed for home and was not to hear from me again for days.

The man who drove me to The Ranch put me at ease. He was also from New England and we were able to talk about what a shame it was that there were no Dunkin

Donuts close by. It was a long ride to The Ranch. When we got there, it was clear I was in the middle of nowhere. This was done on purpose to discourage clients from running away.

My intake to the medical unit took hours. I sat with all of my belongings at my feet, not daring to move. I was so used to psych wards, where if they tell you to sit, you stay there until they tell you to move. Looking back on it, I think it would have been ok to move. I was finally brought to my room. I almost fell over when I saw it. It looked like a bedroom. Not a sterile hospital room. It was a real bedroom with floral print bedding and attached bathroom. I didn't even have to keep my door open to sleep.

The next day, I asked one of the nurses when we were allowed to go outside. She told me that the doors were not locked, I could go outside whenever I wanted as long as I stayed close. I made it to a bench outside the door before I sat down and sobbed. I hadn't been outside in over two weeks. The nurse came to sit with me and I told her why I was crying. She started to cry with me. This same nurse would later on hand me a container of shaping clay to help counteract my anxiety. It worked.

I spent several days inside the medical unit while various therapists met with me to determine where I should be placed. The Ranch was a lot like Harry Potter, you get sorted into houses based on your personality (substance abuse, eating disorder, trauma, codependency). There was some debate to where I should go at first. This is because it took me a few days to admit I had an eating disorder. I was unsure if I was ready and willing to give this part up. After being beaten down by my own exhaustion, I finally admitted to it and was sent to the eating disorder house, Windsong.

The Ranch is set on 2,000 acres, so a van was required to take me to Windsong. The house was huge and set directly next to a horse barn. We could look out and see them during the day. It was also set on a dirt road that we were allowed to limitedly walk up and down. Porches were on both ends of the house with rocking chairs. When I walked into Windsong, the ladies who were already there were doing arts and crafts. One of them, Carson, I had been in the medical unit with. At the time, she had been detoxing and was often nodding out at the dining table. Carson was so happy to see me and said she had told everyone she was hoping it was me, her new friend, coming over to the house.

Carson gave me a tour of Windsong as well as went over some of the rules. The main communal room held: four couches, a TV we could watch only on weekends, a stereo, bookshelf, arts and craft supplies, bins for our makeup and other things we weren't allowed to have in our rooms, a dining table that held more than twenty people, and a smaller table for activities, which could also be utilized by those residents who no longer needed supervised meals. Upstairs were the group rooms and therapist offices. Those doors remained locked. There was also a bathroom which remained locked, and for the first two weeks, a staff member was required to flush the toilet for us. The kitchen, which held double of everything (stove, microwave, freezers, refrigerators), also remained locked unless we were preparing our meals. Bedrooms also had their own bathrooms that remained locked except for certain hours and we were not allowed to hang out in our bedrooms. All meals required very specific planning. We had thirty minutes to prepare the meal, an hour to eat, and thirty minutes after meals (or fifteen for snacks) where we all had to sit in the common area and process how we felt. We were not allowed to get up and there was no bathroom time until it was over. Although the kitchen was huge, getting nearly twenty people in and out was chaos.

The Ranch operated on a phase system, meaning there were certain goals set out as part of treatment and when goals were met, signed off as completed by the staff, and a letter written to request 'phasing up', more privileges were awarded. These included more phone time, going on outings, having use of your cell phone or computer for limited time, etc. The goals included completing meals, running a group, actively participating in your own treatment plan, and following the rules.

I was overwhelmed for the first few days. The schedule was nonstop; from seven in the morning until nine at night, we were doing things. Every day was filled by group therapy, individual therapy, equine therapy, trauma therapy. We also had adventure therapy once a week. Most of the time this was a ropes course, or we went on a walkin meditation. On one of these days, we were encouraged get harnessed in and climb up a forty- foot pole… then off. I was terrified, and I spent the entire time refusin it. After a lot of encouragement and promises that I to climb up a few rungs, I tried it. I got strapp started climbing. I quickly realized that it was rock climbing which I loved. I pretty quickly climbed up the entire pole with the cheers of everyone around me. As soon as I realized what I had just done, dread set in. I wrapped my arms around that pole and yelled down that there was no way I was going to be able to jump off. After many minutes of being told I had no other option, talking through why I was scared, hanging onto the pole like it was my own life, I took a breath, and I let go. It was nothing like flying, I was just falling and screaming. When I reached the ground, I was shaking - which was ok. The second I hit the ground, every single person ran over to me with tears in their eyes to hug me. They told me how amazing it was to watch me, how I just ended up going for it and getting to the top and how letting go after trying to hang on was incredible. The whole point of the exercise was to practice surrender. How fitting that I entered The Ranch struggling to let go of my eating disorder, and once I was willing, I found a group of women to hold me up.

I think equine therapy was similar to this. I was able to do one-on-one sessions. We started out doing an activity, as I continued these sessions, I ended up spending time specific horse. A brown horse with a star on his never told the horses' names. Instead, we them ourselves. Sun and I connected in a understand 'horse people'. He would his mane. I learned to groom the point where I could over and press his nose our foreheads together and that for minutes at a time. This giant animal who could overtake me at any time wanted to be close to me. He would seek me out and we would just be still. I understood this metaphor too. I was supposed to learn that just because I could be hurt, doesn't mean I would be. It required trust.

As it was at Silver Hill, the most important thing that happened while I was at The Ranch were the friendships I made. We were all put together to go into battle against ED. We understood each other without having to say a word. We could talk about it if we wanted to, though. There was always someone willing to listen, always someone who knew how to help if you came back from trauma therapy in a dissociative state. I finally learned that I could have meaningful relationships with women. We have a closed Facebook group, so we can stay in touch with each other. We all use it to keep up to date of our lives, and to virtually come together to show each other support.

I will never, in my whole life, be able to describe how amazing each person I met at The Ranch is. We laughed, we cried, we helped each other, we dyed hair, taught makeup tricks, looked at the stars, hugged, developed lasting relationships. Occasionally, we had a woman's circle where a woman named Blue Heron taught us Native American songs, gave us drums to bang on, and a way to celebrate being female. We howled at the moon to rejoice, threw dance parties on days when things were extra hard.

The staff was also otherworldly. The therapists that I worked with connected with me in ways I never was able to with others. The resident assistants saw us at our worst and our best. God bless them, they still loved us, even when we were yelling or harming ourselves. The campus was so huge that staff also included drivers. One of the drivers was an older man who was so sweet and went out of his way to make sure he could drive me. He would blast songs from his church and sing at the top of his lungs with a smile on his face. Another, I will never be able to forget. She was in recovery from a drug addiction and was a Ranch alumni. She, too, went out of her way to drive me. She even requested to drive me when I went to a step-down program, a program that would be short-lived because I was not ready and slipped right back into my eating disorder. She listened to me state that I wanted to leave, or I wasn't going to go to further treatment because I just wanted to be done. Every time, she would talk to me about all of my options and offered up her wisdom. She understood that most of the time, I was not really listening, I was not ready to. She never gave up. With her persistence, I stayed in treatment longer than I wanted to, and thank goodness I did. It is my belief that she is more responsible for getting me to step up and help myself than anyone else.

The step-down program I went to was also in Tennessee, at a place called Integrative Life Center. The house was beautiful, we had trails in the woods we could walk, and were able to participate in sweat lodges. Some of it was hell. We would have breath work groups, where the whole idea was to sit in a dark room and breathe so we could connect to our bodies. For anyone who has PTSD (which we all did), doing this causes a lot of crying and disassociating. Since it was a step-down program, there was a lot in means of freedom of what we could do. For my birthday, we went to look at Christmas lights. We were allowed cell phones, could go home for holidays. I also made lifelong friends with the people I met here. I was just not ready to do the work needed for the freedom allowed. When I admitted that I was back in my ED behavior, I was quickly moved back to The Ranch.

When I returned, I had already been in treatment for six months. I had left in July and it was now January. At this point, I had so much stuff with me because of the changing seasons. My first experience at The Ranch was so good, I didn't expect any different. I returned to find that the new ladies at Windsong felt threatened by me because I had already been there. The Ranch had also been sold to a big corporation so a lot of changes in the program and the staff had been made. I found that I had a new therapist, even though my pervious one was still there. I put up a lot of resistance and cried during the first Body Image group because it was run by a different person and I was sure the previous person was going to save my life.

Slowly, I warmed up to my new therapist. Thank goodness, because she was exactly what I needed. She was tough on me and I needed tough. I needed someone to call me out on my bullshit. She pushed me to 'phase up' enough that I would be able to go to a walk-a-thon for eating disorder awareness. I didn't want to at first. I was set on staying at the lowest phase and leaving as fast as I could. I didn't. Instead I stayed for three more months. Those months were hard. I missed my first group, but came to love my new sisters just as much. I missed my first therapist, but learned how to expect more from myself with the new one.

It would be a lovely end to say that when I finished my nine months of treatment, I was ready to take on the world with a newfound sense of purpose. I wasn't. Months later, I took the overdose that landed me in a coma for four days. My college roommate had come to visit, and they ended up holding my hand in the emergency room for five hours as a way of saying goodbye from the visit. It changed our relationship and we are still trying to repair it.

Recovery takes a lifetime. Some days, I struggle more than others. New obstacles come up, and I have to rework things, remember all that I have been taught. I am honest about my time in treatment and it is not always met with positive feedback. That's ok, we can only meet people where they are in their own understanding of things. I have had my mental illness thrown back in my face as a reason for why a relationship hasn't worked. While that hurts, I am glad to have figured that out before the relationship got more serious. The people I need in my life will be around. I also have to give people time and understanding when they find out this information. I didn't immediately figure out a way to be okay with all I am up against. I cannot expect it of anyone else. Some days, I think it would be easier to not fight my eating disorder. The easier, softer way is not how I will get better. It is not how I will find freedom and happiness. I am not yet halfway through, and I am already amazed.

Part Four:

Honest, Open, and Willing

4.15.15

I AM GOING to rebuild, reconstruct. From the basement up; a renovation, a revolution of me. I need to do the work now in order to fix me, and I need help. Not every day, not every moment is going to be positive or good. It will be better, it will be forward. I CAN HAVE a job I love, a family, kids, a future. I deserve to be happy. I deserve all the things everyone else does. I am not too much work. I am not too much work. I am not too much work. I am not too much work. I am not too much work. I am not too much work.[19]

---

[19] *You aren't either*

My Gratitude List

Thank you to Sarah Fader, Sarah Comerford, Sparklle Rainne, Christa Marie, and everyone who is a part of Eliezer Tristan Publishing. All of you are doing life changing work. Thank you for letting our stories be heard.

Thank you to Tea Jay and Mariah Ashlyn Elkes, my editors, you put in so much hard work into making this book the best it could be.

Thank you to my family, you have given me my life several times over.

Thank you to Bruce Durand, Kala Farnham, Walter Wright, Natasha Darius, Elizabeth Franz, Luis Romero, Alex Allinson for being such amazing and supportive friends no matter what I am doing.

Thank you, Ashley Flores, for being not only my friend but my family.

Thank you to my theatre family. Your love gives me strength every day.

Thank you to all of my fellow sloth writers, you instantly accepted and supported me. What an incredible group to be weird with.

Thank you to everyone at The Ranch and ILC. Especially Mary Eber and my Windy sisters. You loved me before I could ever love myself.

Thank you to that small voice inside of me that yelled loud enough to keep me going.

References, So I Don't Go to Jail

Anderson, Hans Christian. *The Snow Queen.* The Complete Fairy Tales and Stories trans. Haugaard, Christian, Erik. 1983.

Brown, Brene. *The Power Of Vulnerability.* TEDXHouston, Houston, TX, 2010.

Carle, Eric. The Very Lonely Firefly. Penguin Young Readers Group, 1995.

Clements, Ron. Musker, John. *The Little Mermaid.* Walt Disney Productions, 1989.

Melton, Doyle, Glennon. Carry On Warrior. Scribner, New York, NY.2013.

Melton, Doyle, Glennon. Love Warrior. Flatiron Books, 2016.

Melton, Doyle, Glennon. *Why The World Needs The Mentally Different.* April 13, 2015, http://momastery.com/blog/2015/04/13/world-mentally.

Miranda, Lin-Manuel. *Hamilton.* Public Theatre, New York, NY. 2015.

Rogers, M., Fred. *You Can Never Go Down The Drain.* PBS Kids,1969.

Whitman, Walt. Leaves Of Grass Comprehensive Reader's Edition. New York University Press, 1965.